AFTER ABBEY ROAD

THE SOLO HITS OF THE
BEATLES

GARY FEARON

First printing May 2020

ISBN 978-1-7348555-1-7 (paperback)
ISBN 978-1-7348555-2-4 (digital)
ISBN 978-1-7348555-3-1 (audiobook)

To John, Paul, George and Ringo
for their music and inspiration

And to my fellow Beatlemaniacs
here, there and everywhere

CONTENTS

FOREWORD

It seems unreal that half a century could have come and gone since the Beatles disbanded and went their separate ways. And yet, the echoes of Beatlemania continue to reverberate. No other musical act has come close to rivaling them in terms of commercial success, critical praise, and lasting impact on music and culture.

By the time Paul McCartney issued a press release announcing he was leaving the group in April 1970, each of the Beatles had already "quit" at one time or another, only to return days later. When their final album *Let It Be* was released in May, fans were already accustomed to their solo intentions thanks to several singles by John Lennon as well as Paul's debut album *McCartney*. Ringo Starr would soon make a statement with his own LP, followed by a chart-topping triple album set by George Harrison.

From 1962 to 1970, the Beatles released around 200 songs and two dozen singles. As solo artists, they have since issued nearly a thousand more recordings between them. Of these, well over 200 have been chosen as singles. These songs, considered to be the best of the best, not only provide a more precise showcase for the talents of each ex-Beatle, but magnify the individual genius they contributed to the most acclaimed group of all time.

Much has been told about The Beatles' classic hits and the inspiration behind them. Such legends as that of the school drawing by Julian Lennon that led to "Lucy in the Sky with Diamonds" or Paul's dream melody that prompted "Yesterday" have been fascinating insights into the creative process. The goal of *After Abbey Road* is to continue that study and reveal the equally intriguing stories behind all fifty years of their solo singles.

The songs are presented here in order of their earliest release as singles, offering a side-by-side chronology of the musical life and times of John, Paul, George and Ringo as solo artists. At the time of this writing, every song mentioned can be found on YouTube as well as various streaming sites. And, because the Beatles were innovators in music videos long before MTV came along, a great many of these songs can be seen as well as heard. As you follow along, I encourage you to listen with fresh ears to each one. Knowing the stories behind the songs, you'll have a new appreciation and an even greater respect for the wizardry behind the curtain.

In Beatle days, it was common for a single not to be part of an album. It would instead be a separate entity between LP releases. Sometimes, the solo Beatles continued that practice. Only in later greatest hits collections or as bonus tracks were these released as part of an album. For CD collectors, I have indicated the album on which each song is most readily available.

Because musical tastes can vary from country to country, some songs were released as singles only in America, or the UK, or certain other countries. Thus, songs that may only be known as album cuts to some fans may have been huge hits elsewhere. Additionally, some album cuts were released as promotional singles only to radio stations or club DJs. If they were deemed worthy of a single somewhere, they're included here.

In providing the recording dates of each song, the focus is on when the initial session took place. Many songs involved overdubs weeks or even months later, and that is indicated when significant.

The singer and musician credits tell a story in their own right, underscoring how often close friends and/or virtuosos from other musical genres were partners in creating these hits. String quartets and orchestras were frequently involved but generally not identified. Certain other musician credits and recording dates are unconfirmable and thus excluded in the interests of accuracy.

Lastly, since Paul and Ringo both have been knighted at Buckingham Palace, it would be appropriate to refer to them as Sir Paul and Sir Richard. But, as many times as they are mentioned in this book, that would be overkill, plus they themselves discourage such pomp. It's really for formal occasions anyway, and we're among friends here.

The larger-than-life legacy of the Beatles and their music is filled with conjecture, rumor and exaggeration, and the music they've created as solo artists has been no less open to interpretation. It is my goal in *After Abbey Road* to provide the most accurate, insightful and entertaining details about each single.

Hopefully, this guide will enhance your listening pleasure when revisiting the songs you already know and love, as well as help you discover new treasures you may have missed the first time around. Thank you for joining me on this magical musical tour.

G.F.
May 2020

1. GIVE PEACE A CHANCE
Plastic Ono Band

Written by John Lennon
Recorded June 1, 1969
Released July 4, 1969
Album: POWER TO THE PEOPLE – THE HITS

Both Paul McCartney and John Lennon got married within a week of each other in March 1969. John and his second wife Yoko Ono had hoped to be wed at sea en route to Paris, but because they weren't French citizens, red tape put an end to that plan. Instead, they tied the knot in Gibraltar. Knowing anything they did would make headlines, they used their honeymoon to stage a "bed-in for peace" at the Amsterdam Hilton. Their newlywed misadventures were immortalized in "The Ballad of John and Yoko", recorded by John and Paul the following month.

In June, taking a break from recording sessions for *Abbey Road*, John and Yoko staged another bed-in at the Queen Elizabeth Hotel in Montreal, Quebec, this time arranging to have microphones and a four-track recorder in their room to capture their new anthem "Give Peace a Chance". Visiting celebrities sang and played along, with a thumping rhythm achieved by opening and closing a wardrobe door. Additional voices were overdubbed later.

The simple, two-chord song quickly became the favorite chant of anti-Vietnam war protestors. Though Paul wasn't involved, John gave songwriting credit to Lennon/McCartney, as they had always done from the beginning of their partnership. John later expressed regret for not giving it to Yoko.

John Lennon – vocals, acoustic guitar
Yoko Ono – backing vocals, tambourine, handclaps
Tommy Smothers – acoustic guitar
Radha Krishna Temple, Canada – backing vocals, percussion
Petula Clark, Timothy Leary, Allen Ginsberg, Derek Taylor, Dick
    Gregory, Murray the K, others – backing vocals
André Perry – percussion

2. COLD TURKEY
Plastic Ono Band

Written by John Lennon
Recorded September 30, 1969
Released October 20, 1969
Album: POWER TO THE PEOPLE – THE HITS

During their early days performing all-nighters in Hamburg, the Beatles became well acquainted with amphetamines. When the youth drug culture exploded in the '60s, they expanded their recreational repertoire to marijuana and LSD. But only John took it to the extreme with heroin. He and Yoko became addicted, contributing to episodes of paranoia and volatile outbursts in the studio. With few withdrawal treatment options available, John attempted to quit on his own, and chronicled his painful experiences in "Cold Turkey".

He had hoped to include the song on *Abbey Road*. However, while the Beatles had previously injected subtle drug references into songs like "Got to Get You Into My Life", "With a Little Help from My Friends" and "Happiness is a Warm Gun", this ode to opiate withdrawal was considered too blatant by his bandmates, particularly Paul, always mindful of the group's image. So, John formed his own ensemble to record it, again under the umbrella name Plastic Ono Band.

His fellow Beatles weren't the only ones to reject "Cold Turkey". Radio stations refused to play it because of its drug content. Later that year, when John famously sent back the M.B.E. badge awarded to him in 1965 by Queen Elizabeth, he told Her Majesty, "I am returning this M.B.E. in protest against Britain's involvement in the Nigeria-Biafra thing, against our support of America in Vietnam, and against 'Cold Turkey' slipping down the charts."

John Lennon – vocals, electric guitar
Eric Clapton – electric guitar
Klaus Voorman – bass guitar
Ringo Starr – drums

3. INSTANT KARMA! (WE ALL SHINE ON)
Lennon/Ono with the Plastic Ono Band

Written by John Lennon
Recorded January 27, 1970
Released February 6, 1970
Album: POWER TO THE PEOPLE – THE HITS

In January 1970, while John and Yoko visited Yoko's ex-husband Tony Cox in Denmark, conversation topics included the theory of "instant karma," in which the poetic justice of one's actions occur immediately rather than over time. Two days after returning to England, John woke up with the inklings of a song inspired by the concept. At his piano, he finished writing "Instant Karma!" in an hour. In his eagerness to record it, he called producer Phil Spector and said, "Come over to Apple quick, I've just written a monster."

John wanted Spector to give it his trademark "wall of sound" as heard on songs he had produced for The Ronettes and The Righteous Brothers. Consequently, multiple pianos and extreme echo were included in the drum-heavy track. When more backup singers were needed, they went to a nearby club and enlisted additional voices.

"Instant Karma!" was released and on the radio just ten days after it was written. John quipped at the time that he "wrote it for breakfast, recorded it for lunch, and we're putting it out for dinner."

Horror author Stephen King said the chorus phrase "We all shine on" inspired the title of his 1977 novel *The Shining*.

John Lennon – lead vocal, acoustic guitar, piano
Yoko Ono – backing vocals
George Harrison – electric guitar, piano, backing vocals
Klaus Voorman – bass guitar, electric piano, backing vocals
Billy Preston – Hammond organ, backing vocals
Alan White – drums, piano, backing vocals
Mal Evans – chimes, handclaps, backing vocals
Allen Klein – backing vocals
Singers recruited from the Hatchett Club – backing vocals

4. BEAUCOUPS OF BLUES
Ringo Starr

Written by Buzz Rabin
Recorded June 30, 1970
Released: October 5, 1970
Album: BEAUCOUPS OF BLUES

Following the Beatles' breakup, it's likely that Ringo Starr would have focused on his non-musical interests, particularly filmmaking and acting, had it not been for the encouragement of his bandmates, who suggested he record a solo album. His first release, *Sentimental Journey*, was a collection of standards chosen to honor his parents and his older relatives, who were his first musical influences. Beatles producer George Martin oversaw the recording sessions, and Paul McCartney contributed an arrangement of "Stardust". Though well-received, *Sentimental Journey* yielded no singles.

Later in 1970, Ringo released a second album, *Beaucoups of Blues*, a country collection well-suited to his melancholy voice. Pete Drake, a renowned pedal steel guitarist who had performed on such hits as "Rose Garden", "Behind Closed Doors" and "Stand by Your Man" was the producer. Drake was working with George Harrison on his upcoming solo album *All Things Must Pass* when Ringo, a longtime country fan, asked Drake to collaborate on an album.

Written by Nashville songwriters, the songs on *Beaucoups of Blues* were handpicked from demos and recorded in just two days' time. The title track, penned by Buzz Rabin and released as Ringo's first solo single, was inspired by Rabin's teenage years in Louisiana, where he remembered people saying "beaucoups of this and beaucoups of that."

Backup vocals were provided by The Jordanaires of Elvis fame.

Ringo Starr – vocals, drums
The Jordanaires – backing vocals
Charlie McCoy – harmonica
Roy Huskey, Jr. – upright bass
Session musicians – guitar, pedal steel guitar, fiddle

5. MY SWEET LORD
George Harrison

Written by George Harrison
Recorded May–October 1970
Released November 23, 1970
Album: ALL THINGS MUST PASS

Impressed with Phil Spector's production of John's "Instant Karma!", George Harrison enlisted Spector to produce his solo album *All Things Must Pass*. The backlog of songs George had written but hadn't been able to record with the Beatles helped to make it a triple-album set, the first ever released by a solo artist. It enjoyed many weeks at the top of the album charts.

George was on tour in Europe when he came up with the idea for his most successful solo single, "My Sweet Lord". Inspired by the sound of the Edwin Hawkins Singers' version of "Oh Happy Day", his devotional song interspersed the Christian and Hindu praise phrases "Hallelujah" and "Hare Krishna" throughout. It also debuted the slide guitar sound that became a Harrison trademark.

"My Sweet Lord" was the first post-Beatles single to reach #1. It was still on the charts when Bright Tunes, publisher of the Chiffons' 1963 hit "He's So Fine", filed a lawsuit against George claiming copyright infringement. The similarities were unintentional but undeniable. The court found George guilty of "subconscious plagiarism." After years of litigation, he would settle the suit for $587,000 and purchase the copyright to "He's So Fine."

George Harrison – lead vocals, acoustic guitar, slide guitar
Eric Clapton – guitar, backing vocals
Peter Frampton, Pete Ham, Tom Evans, Joey Molland – guitars
Billy Preston – piano, backing vocals
Gary Wright – electric piano
Klaus Voorman – bass guitar
Ringo Starr, Jim Gordon, Mike Gibbins – drums and percussion
Bobby Whitlock – harmonium, backing vocals
Phil Spector – backup vocals

6. MOTHER
John Lennon

Written by John Lennon
Recorded September–October 1970
Released December 28, 1970
Album: JOHN LENNON/PLASTIC ONO BAND

While watching a horror movie on TV, John took note of some dark, mysterious-sounding bells on the soundtrack, and decided that's how his new album should begin. So "Mother", the opening track on *John Lennon/Plastic Ono Band*, starts with four painfully slowed-down peals of a funeral bell, aptly foreshadowing the dramatic, raw emotions that follow. The somber intro on this, his first solo album to crack Billboard's Top 100, symbolizes the death of his former life with the Beatles. The single release of "Mother" for radio play ran considerably shorter by editing out the opening bells.

Written after undergoing four months of primal therapy with psychotherapist Arthur Janov in Los Angeles, the song reflects the treatment's goal of expressing long-repressed childhood pain, which John had his share of. His mother Julia was killed by a drunk driver when he was 17, and his father Alfred abandoned the family many years prior. In "Mother" he resigns himself to telling them goodbye.

The bare bones production of piano, bass and drums sets an uncluttered stage for John's impassioned vocals. His repeated coda of "Mama don't go, Daddy come home" is delivered in primal screams characteristic of Janov's therapy. John recorded them via multiple takes in the evenings, after the rest of the day's recordings were done, so as not to ruin his voice.

In contrast to this potent opening song, he closed the album with the gentle, nursery rhyme-like "My Mummy's Dead", delivered with a voice emptied of emotion.

John Lennon – vocals, piano
Ringo Starr – drums
Klaus Voorman – bass guitar

7. WHAT IS LIFE
George Harrison

Written by George Harrison
Recorded May–June 1970
Released February 15, 1971
Album: ALL THINGS MUST PASS

Written while still a member of the Beatles, George came up with "What is Life" while driving to a London recording session for Billy Preston. He wrote the song quickly and had originally intended to give it to his fellow Apple Records artist to record, but upon arriving at the studio, he concluded that it didn't fit in with the "funky stuff" Preston was working on.

Featuring a fuzz guitar riff played by George, the joyful, Motownesque "What is Life" explores not the meaning of life, but how life would be meaningless without love. Like many of his post-Beatles love songs, it expresses a devotion that could be just as easily about a higher power as about a girl, a devotion both universal and individual.

Along with most of the songs on *All Things Must Pass*, it featured Phil Spector's wall of sound with multiple guitars playing the same parts and George doing his own harmonies. In retrospect, George felt there was "too much echo" added to the final product, so it was remixed for its 2001 CD rerelease.

Among the musicians backing him up were the members of the band Badfinger, whose hits include "Day After Day", a song George went on to produce.

George Harrison – vocals, guitar
Eric Clapton, Pete Ham, Tom Evans, Joey Molland – guitars
Carl Radle – bass guitar
Bobby Whitlock – piano
Jim Gordon – drums
Bobby Keys – saxophone
Jim Price – trumpet
Mike Gibbins – tambourine

8. ANOTHER DAY
Paul McCartney

Written by Paul McCartney
Recorded October 1970–January 1971
Released February 19, 1971
Album: WINGS GREATEST

Paul McCartney was the last Beatle to put out a solo single, but the first Beatle to publicly announce he was quitting the group. He made the proclamation in the press release for his April 1970 solo album, *McCartney*. Performing all of the instruments, Paul made it a solo album in every sense of the word. No singles were chosen from that LP, although "Maybe I'm Amazed" received significant album play on many radio stations.

For his second album, he brought in session musicians to assist after holding clandestine New York auditions rumored to be for an advertising jingle. Guitarist David Spinozza and drummer Denny Seiwell were hired, the latter of whom would soon join the first incarnation of Paul's group Wings.

Intent on creating a unique musical identity distinct from that of the Beatles, Paul also engaged his wife Linda to sing harmonies and began giving her keyboard lessons.

Originally intended for a Beatles album, "Another Day" was the first song recorded for Paul's sophomore project *Ram*. Instead, it was released as a single and became a top ten hit worldwide.

The third-person lyrics convey the life of a lonely woman who goes through the motions of a monotonous existence. Her only escape comes from stolen hours with a man who won't commit and sometimes stands her up. When McCartney presented "Another Day" to his musicians, David Spinozza affectionately referred to the song as "Eleanor Rigby in New York."

Paul McCartney – vocals, bass guitar, acoustic guitar, shaker
Linda McCartney – backing vocals
David Spinozza – electric guitar
Denny Seiwell – drums, percussion

9. POWER TO THE PEOPLE
John Lennon/Plastic Ono Band

Written by John Lennon
Recorded January 22–February 9, 1971
Released March 12, 1971
Album: POWER TO THE PEOPLE – THE HITS

In the late sixties, John was given a supply of military clothing by an ex-Army man who wanted the items to be used for art or some other cause. Subsequently, John and Yoko began wearing militant garb, a fashion statement that went well with their reputation as revolutionaries. Their rebel stance was particularly evident on John's fifth solo single, "Power to the People".

Written quickly and triggered by criticism over his and Yoko's "passive" publicity stunts to promote peace, the song was intended to be a more radical anthem for crowds to chant. What "Give Peace a Chance" did for the peace movement, "Power to the People" was to do for political activism. Instead of a bed-in, the message was now "get on your feet and into the street." To drive the point home, the sound of marching was added to the intro, replicating the atmosphere of a demonstration.

A few years later, John revealed that he hadn't been thinking clearly at the time and wrote "Power to the People" to appease the antiestablishment crowd who "hated anyone who wasn't poor" and expected him and Yoko to feel the same. In his book *Skywriting by Word of Mouth*, John dismissed the song as "rather embarrassing" and "ten years too late."

Among the backup singers was Rosetta Hightower of The Orlons ("South Street"), who had backed up numerous other artists as diverse as Bobby Rydell and Joe Cocker.

John Lennon – vocals, piano
Rosetta Hightower and others – backing vocals, handclaps
Klaus Voorman – bass
Jim Gordon – drums
Bobby Keys – saxophone

10. IT DON'T COME EASY
Ringo Starr

Written by Richard Starkey and George Harrison
Recorded March 8–11, 1971
Released April 9, 1971
Album: RINGO

Originally titled "Gotta Pay Your Dues", George Harrison wrote this song and offered it to Badfinger, but they opted instead to sing backup on Ringo's rendition, "It Don't Come Easy".

While collaborating on the song with Ringo, George suggested that the last verse be about God, but Starr resisted. George then pushed for Krishna. Ringo protested further, and they eventually agreed on peace as the focal point for the final verse. But George still got his Hare Krishna in, by means of backup vocals during the instrumental break.

The distinctive flanging effect heard on George's guitar was accomplished by running it through a rotating Leslie speaker cabinet, normally reserved for organ.

Though "It Don't Come Easy" suggests struggle, it offers the solution of "peace and love," which would become Ringo's catchphrase throughout his solo career. With lyrics about forgetting sorrows of the past and an admonishment to "come together," it was seen as an olive branch from Ringo and George toward John and Paul, all of whom were still dealing with arbitration and misgivings following the band's breakup.

Ringo Starr – vocals, drums
George Harrison – guitars
Stephen Stills – piano
Gary Wright – organ
Klaus Voorman – bass guitar
Pete Ham, Tom Evans – backing vocals
Ron Cattermole – saxophone, trumpet
Mal Evans – tambourine
Jim Keltner – maracas

11. BANGLADESH
George Harrison

Written by George Harrison
Recorded July 1971
Released July 28, 1971
Album: LIVING IN THE MATERIAL WORLD

While filming the Beatles movie *Help!* in 1965, one of the props on the set was a sitar that George fiddled with. He bought one of his own later that year, which he used to play the first sitar solo to appear on a pop record ("Norwegian Wood"). His eagerness to become more proficient on the complex Indian instrument led him to sitar master Ravi Shankar, who gave George private lessons. The two became lifelong friends.

By 1971, East Pakistan was experiencing a refugee crisis following political unrest and disastrous flooding that left millions lacking in food and water. Shankar, hoping to bring the plight of Bangladesh to the world's attention, asked for George's help. He said he'd make a few calls. Those calls resulted in two giant fundraiser concerts at Madison Square Garden on August 1, 1971.

Led by George, the star-studded lineup included Bob Dylan, Leon Russell and Billy Preston as well as Ringo Starr, marking the first time two ex-Beatles appeared on the same stage together. "The Concert for Bangladesh" was a groundbreaking event that paved the way for future relief efforts to come, including Live Aid, Band Aid and Farm Aid.

As for the titular song, George wrote it at the piano "in less than ten minutes." He rush-released this studio version of "Bangladesh" three days before the concerts.

George Harrison – vocals, electric guitar, slide guitar
Leon Russell – piano
Billy Preston – organ
Klaus Voorman – bass
Ringo Starr, Jim Keltner – drums
Jim Horn – tenor saxophone, baritone saxophone

12. UNCLE ALBERT/ADMIRAL HALSEY
Paul and Linda McCartney

Written by Paul and Linda McCartney
Recorded November 1970–April 1971
Released May 21, 1971
Album: RAM

Albert Kendall worked with Paul's father Jim as a clerk at Liverpool cotton merchant A. Hanney & Co., and eventually married Paul's Aunt Milly. Albert quoted the Bible when he was drunk and was "a lot of fun," said Paul. While writing "Uncle Albert", Paul felt nostalgic and spoke of it as an apology to the older generation for how unsettling the world must have become for them, not least of all because of the contributions of his own generation.

The song's other namesake bears an allusion to WWII U.S. Naval officer Fleet Admiral William "Bull" Halsey, a commander in the South Pacific, who in 1944 led his fleet into what became known as Typhoon Halsey, a storm that sank ships and aircraft and claimed the lives of over 800 seamen.

"Uncle Albert/Admiral Halsey" contains two other song fragments merged in best *Abbey Road* medley style: "Hands Across the Water" and "Get Around". The frequently changing sonic landscape includes sound effects of thunder and rain and Paul imitating a telephone, while he and Linda provide a variety of English accents. The "butter pie" mentioned during one of their exchanges is a potato and onion pie native to Lancashire. The dish is also known as "Catholic Pie" because it was created as a non-meat alternative for Fridays.

Released as a single in America, "Uncle Albert/Admiral Halsey" became Paul's first #1 hit and first gold record as a solo artist.

Paul McCartney – vocals, guitars, piano, bass, xylophone
Linda McCartney – backing vocals
David Spinozza, Hugh McCracken – guitars
Denny Seiwell – drums, percussion
Marvin Stamm – flugelhorn

13. BACK SEAT OF MY CAR
Paul and Linda McCartney

Written by Paul and Linda McCartney
Recorded October 22, 1970
Released August 13, 1971
Album: RAM

This closing song on *Ram* was inspired by long road trips Paul and Linda were fond of taking as an escape during the Beatles' breakup. Written as an ode to amorous teenage defiance, "Back Seat of My Car" is from the viewpoint of a young couple taking to the road and dismissing the moral advice of the girl's parents.

Originally intended for a Beatles album, "Back Seat of My Car" features a lush arrangement and soaring vocals that suggest the influence of Brian Wilson, a McCartney favorite whose own songs frequently immortalized the teenage experience, as well as cars.

Paul's interest in classical music is also evident in both the string arrangement and the use of changing and recurring themes that weave in and out throughout the song. As he had done on "Uncle Albert/Admiral Halsey" and other *Ram* songs, Paul did the orchestral arrangement and conducted the New York Philharmonic. A surprising number of the orchestra members didn't know who Paul McCartney was, being strictly classical musicians.

During the early '70s, Paul and John were taking the occasional musical potshot at each other, with Paul deriding John's penchant for telling people what to do ("Too Many People"), and John accusing Paul of writing lukewarm music ("How Do You Sleep"). Reportedly, John felt that the oft-repeated line "we believe that we can't be wrong" in "Back Seat of My Car" was directed at him and Yoko.

Paul McCartney – vocals, piano, guitar, bass guitar
Linda McCartney – backing vocals
David Spinozza – lead guitar
Hugh McCracken – lead guitar
Denny Seiwell – drums

14. EAT AT HOME
Paul and Linda McCartney

Written by Paul and Linda McCartney
Recorded October 18, 1970
Released 1971
Album: RAM

While "Uncle Albert/Admiral Halsey" was released as a single only in America, and "Back Seat of My Car" was released only in the UK, Paul and Linda's "Eat at Home" was the single chosen for Australia, New Zealand, South America, Japan, and the European audience.

Each of the Beatles had been Buddy Holly fans. Paul and John were inspired to start writing songs after learning that Holly was not just a singer but also a writer. They recorded his "Words of Love" on one of their albums. And, of course, The Beatles' very name was a takeoff on Holly's group The Crickets. Holly's influence can be heard on the *Ram* rocker "Eat at Home", from Paul's vocal affectations on words like "lady" to the long Holly-like hiccups on "love." The song is largely built around three chords, characteristic of the Holly heyday. Though John was critical of the songs on *Ram*, he openly admitted that he liked "Eat at Home".

Praising home and hearth, cooking and sex, "Eat at Home" was one of many McCartney songs that would testify to Paul and Linda's post-Beatle domestic bliss. With a renovated farmhouse in Scotland to retreat to and their second child together (Stella) on the way, the McCartneys in 1971 maintained as normal a family life as their superstar status would allow.

That same year, Paul founded McCartney Publishing, Ltd. (MPL Communications), which would purchase the copyrights to Buddy Holly's song catalog along with the works of numerous other composers.

Paul McCartney – vocals, electric guitar, bass guitar, drums
Linda McCartney – backing vocals
David Spinozza – lead guitar
Denny Seiwell – drums

15. IMAGINE
John Lennon

Written by John Lennon
Recorded May 27, 1971
Released October 11, 1971
Album: IMAGINE

The title track from John's second solo album became his first #1 single and his signature song as a solo artist.

Its origin can be traced to Yoko Ono's 1964 poetry book *Grapefruit*, which entertained a variety of imaginings. The back cover of the *Imagine* album quotes Ono's poem "Cloud Piece":

Imagine the clouds dripping.
Dig a hole in your garden to put them in.

Playing an equally significant role in the creative process was an inspirational book given to John and Yoko by activist Dick Gregory on the power of positive prayer.

Written one morning in early 1971 in his bedroom in Ascot, Berkshire, England, John nearly completed the song during the same short session. It was recorded just as efficiently at his new home studio, using the second of only three takes. Strings were added later in America by the New York Philharmonic, the same orchestra Paul had hired for *Ram*. The liner notes on *Imagine* identified them as "The Flux Fiddlers."

In contrast to the "wall of sound" heard on previous Lennon singles, the production was as simple as the message itself: a world without conflict would be a world with peace. John said "Imagine" was a way of getting a controversial message across "with a little honey."

John considered it as strong a song as any he had written as a Beatle. Paul said he knew it was "a killer" the first time he heard it.

John Lennon – vocals, piano
Klaus Voorman – electric bass
Alan White – drums
The Flux Fiddlers – strings

16. HAPPY XMAS (WAR IS OVER)
John & Yoko/Plastic Ono Band

Written by John Lennon and Yoko Ono
Recorded October 28, 1971
Released December 1, 1971
Album: IMAGINE

Each Christmas from 1963 to 1969, The Beatles recorded festive holiday records for members of their official fan club. After the group's 1970 breakup, John was the first ex-Beatle to release a Christmas single for the general public. George, Paul and Ringo would all follow suit in the years to come.

Not unlike "Imagine" with its "believe it and you can get it" precept, "Happy Xmas (War is Over)" continued John and Yoko's musical crusade for world peace. The title echoes a billboard campaign they had done in 1969.

John said he wrote it because he was "sick of 'White Christmas'" and hoped his song would become a new anthem for the holiday season. In keeping with the yuletide spirit, the 7" single of "Happy Xmas (War is Over)" was released on green vinyl.

One of the guitarists on the session was Hugh McCracken, who, unbeknownst to John, was the lead guitarist on Paul McCartney's latest album. Fearing it might result in his ouster, McCracken tried to keep it quiet. When John did find out who he was, he lightened the atmosphere by joking that Hugh was just auditioning on *Ram*.

John Lennon – vocals, guitar
Yoko Ono – vocals
The Harlem Community Choir – children's chorus
May Pang – backing vocals
Nicky Hopkins – piano, glockenspiel, chimes
Jim Keltner – drums, sleigh bells
Hugh McCracken – guitar
Teddy Irwin – guitar
Chris Osbourne – guitar
Stuart Scharf – guitar

17. GIVE IRELAND BACK TO THE IRISH
Wings

Written by Paul and Linda McCartney
Recorded February 1, 1972
Released February 25, 1972
Album: WINGS WILD LIFE

Paul's first session at Abbey Road Studios since the Beatles' breakup was prompted by world events. On January 30, 1972, British soldiers shot and killed 13 unarmed protesters in Northern Ireland, an incident that became known as Bloody Sunday. Two days later, Paul and his newly formed band Wings recorded this song in response, essentially asking Great Britain, "What are we doing there?"

Paul anticipated backlash, and it didn't take long to get it. Shortly after submitting the recording to EMI, the chairman of the record company called him to say it was too inflammatory and that they wouldn't release it. Paul demanded that it be released, and it was. "Give Ireland Back to the Irish" was banned in the UK by the BBC but reached #1 in Ireland.

The single marked the debut of Wings' new lead guitarist Henry McCullough, an Irishman himself and a former member of Joe Cocker's backup band. Because of his involvement with "Give Ireland Back to the Irish", McCullough's brother Samuel was beaten up by expatriates in an Irish pub.

Putting out a song with a controversial message was a distinctively John and Yoko move and was regarded by some music critics as an attempt by Paul to give his new band credibility. Political pundits vilified him for what they felt was a show of support for the Irish Republican Army. Paul responded that he wasn't normally into protest songs and wouldn't make a habit of it.

Paul McCartney – vocals, electric bass
Linda McCartney – backing vocals, piano
Denny Laine – backing vocals, guitars
Henry McCullough – lead guitar
Denny Seiwell – drums

18. BACK OFF BOOGALOO
Ringo Starr

Written by Richard Starkey and George Harrison
Recorded September 1971
Released March 17, 1972
Album: BLAST FROM YOUR PAST

The long arm of the Beatles' company Apple Corps extended far beyond music, reaching into such ventures as publishing, electronics and movie production. By 1971, Ringo was spending considerable time at the offices of Apple Films with his friends Marc Bolan of T Rex and Harry Nilsson, both of whom he would soon collaborate with on cinematic projects.

During dinner one evening at Ringo's home, an animated Bolan used the word "boogaloo" so much that it played back as a loop in Ringo's head overnight to the point where a beat and a melody came with it. So as not to forget the catchy song that was forming, Ringo grabbed his portable tape recorder. Discovering that the batteries were dead, he borrowed some from his children's toys.

Because of the song's strong association with Bolan, T Rex fans contended that it was co-written with the glam rock star. However, Ringo brought the basic song to George Harrison, who finished the melody and added some chord changes. "Back Off Boogaloo" was offered to Cilla Black to sing, but she declined. George produced Ringo's version, contributing slide guitar as well.

The line "give me something tasty" came to Ringo while watching a football game on TV. The commentator, Jimmy Hill, would often refer to a player's performance as "tasty."

Ringo Starr – vocals, drums, percussion
George Harrison – slide guitar, acoustic guitar
Gary Wright – piano
Klaus Voorman – electric bass, saxophone
Madeline Bell – backing vocals
Lesley Duncan – backing vocals
Jean Gilbert – backing vocals

19. WOMAN IS THE NIGGER OF THE WORLD
John Lennon/Plastic Ono Band
with Elephant's Memory and Invisible Strings

Written by John Lennon and Yoko Ono
Recorded March 1972
Released April 24, 1972
Album: SOME TIME IN NEW YORK CITY

Emboldened by the success of *Imagine*, John went bigger and brasher with his next album, taking on the most provocative topics of the day. *Some Time in New York City* featured lyrical reproofs about political imprisonment, Attica, marijuana, Bloody Sunday, and the education system. But nothing on the album offended like "Woman is the Nigger of the World", released as a single only in the U.S.

Praised by the National Organization for Women for its message of empowerment, the song was received by most others as a career mistake. Despite an aggressive promotional push, radio stations refused to play it, and it would become John's biggest misstep as a recording artist.

In interviews, the Lennons attempted to explain that they were not trying to promote a racial slur and that the title was in fact inspired by Irish leader James Connolly, who said "the female worker is the slave of the slave." Yoko, who John called a red-hot feminist, had reworded the quote in her own irrepressible style.

Not since John's infamous 1966 "bigger than Jesus" comment had he experienced such backlash. As he had done back then, he stopped performing in public.

John Lennon – vocals, guitar
Wayne Gabriel – guitar
Adam Ippolito – piano
Stan Bronstein – saxophone
Gary Van Scyoc – bass
Jim Keltner – drums
Richard Frank, Jr. – drums, percussion
The Invisible Strings – strings

20. MARY HAD A LITTLE LAMB
Wings

Written by Paul McCartney (lyrics by Sarah Josepha Hale)
Recorded March 1972
Released May 12, 1972
Album: RED ROSE SPEEDWAY

The most celebrated early recording of the human voice occurred in 1877, with Thomas Edison reciting the nursery rhyme "Mary Had a Little Lamb". Because it was the first phonograph recording, Paul wanted to record his own performance of it.

Paul wrote an entirely new melody and chord progression for Sarah Josepha Hale's 1830 poem which, legend has it, was based on a true story. In it, a young girl named Mary Sawyer brought her pet lamb to school in Sudbury, Massachusetts, creating a stir among the students.

The Beatles were known for regularly stepping out of any expected confines, and Paul ensured that Wings would be no less unpredictable. "One minute I might be doing 'Ireland' and the next I'll be doing 'Mary Had a Little Lamb'. I can see how that would look from the sidelines, but the thing is we're not either of those records, but we are both of them."

After his politically polarizing "Give Ireland Back to the Irish", Paul's kid-friendly "Mary Had a Little Lamb" seemed like an inside joke in retaliation for criticism he had received for Wings' last single. But, as he explained, he now had three children and wanted to come up with a good pop song for kids. On top of that, his 2½-year-old daughter Mary enjoyed hearing him sing her name. Appropriately, she and her half-sister Heather can be heard singing backup.

Paul McCartney – vocals, piano, bass
Linda McCartney – vocals
Henry McCullough – mandolin
Denny Laine – guitar
Denny Seiwell – drums
Heather McCartney, Mary McCartney – backing vocals

21. HI HI HI
Wings

Written by Paul and Linda McCartney
Recorded November 1972
Released December 1, 1972
Album: WINGS GREATEST

The third single released in 1972 by Paul was also his second to be blacklisted by the BBC. Written in Spain as an upbeat closer for Wings' live concerts, "Hi Hi Hi" contained enough suggestion of drugs and sex to be deemed unfit for airplay.

Fans accustomed to the innocence of "Mary Had a Little Lamb" were unprepared for this relentless rocker that seemed intent on pushing the envelope. As for Paul, the ban took him by surprise, having intentionally kept certain lyrics ambiguous and open to interpretation. He asserted that Bob Dylan's 1966 hit "Rainy Day Women #12 and 35" had escaped censorship, since "Everybody must get stoned" could be construed in different ways.

Ironically, Paul said that a mistake made by his publishing company is what initially raised the broadcast company's eyebrows. His lyric "Get you ready for my polygon" was intended to be vague innuendo, but Northern Songs transcribed it and sent it out as "Get you ready for my body gun." A frustrated McCartney quipped that those might even be better lyrics.

In live concert, meanwhile, it makes for a great announcement, Paul proudly proclaims. "You can say 'This one was banned!' and everyone goes 'Hooray!' Everyone's a bit anti-all that banning, all that censorship."

Henry McCullough remembers that the unforgiving guitar riff of "Hi Hi Hi" was particularly tricky and took about 50 takes to nail.

Paul McCartney – vocals, electric guitar, electric bass
Linda McCartney – vocals, organ
Denny Laine – vocals, guitar
Henry McCullough – electric guitar
Denny Seiwell – drums, cowbell

22. MY LOVE
Paul McCartney and Wings

Written by Paul and Linda McCartney
Recorded October 1972
Released March 23, 1973
Album: RED ROSE SPEEDWAY

Red Rose Speedway, Paul's fifth album as an ex-Beatle, featured this romantic ballad that became another McCartney standard, soon to be covered by numerous other recording artists from Tony Bennett to Cher. "My Love" was Paul's first solo hit worldwide.

Written several years prior, Paul wanted to give "My Love" special treatment. He commissioned a 50-piece orchestra with jazz experience to lend the song a certain torch song/lounge-music feel. Alongside Wings, they recorded twenty live takes over a three-hour session, finally pleading with Paul that they couldn't give him any more of what he wanted than they already had.

The famous guitar solo was not only one of the song's highlights, but a coup for Henry McCullough. Up to that point, Paul instructed his band members on every note to play. As an established guitarist of some repute, McCullough didn't like being restricted to the solo Paul had written. When McCullough asked if he could try something else, Paul was hesitant but he consented, and the result was an instant triumph. McCullough considered the solo the best of his career, and Paul has declared "My Love" his favorite song from the Wings years.

In addition to this lush ballad written for Linda, *Red Rose Speedway* contained another personalized expression of affection. Embossed on the back cover, in Braille, were the words "We love you Baby", a message meant for the McCartneys' friend Stevie Wonder.

Paul McCartney – vocals, electric piano
Linda McCartney – backing vocals
Denny Laine – backing vocals, electric bass
Henry McCullough – lead guitar
Denny Seiwell – drums

23. GIVE ME LOVE (GIVE ME PEACE ON EARTH)
George Harrison

Written by George Harrison
Recorded Fall 1972
Released May 7, 1973
Album: LIVING IN THE MATERIAL WORLD

Two years had passed since the success of his critically acclaimed triple album *All Things Must Pass*, and George was ready to get back in the studio. He had intended to work with producer Phil Spector again. However, the eccentric Spector was proving to be unreliable, so George produced his next album, *Living in the Material World*, by himself. The only single released from it, "Give Me Love (Give Me Peace on Earth)", became another international hit.

One of several songs on *Material World* that centered around spiritual concepts and phrases, George called this prayerful plea "a personal statement between me, the Lord, and whoever likes it." The lyric "keep me free from birth" reflected George's Hindu beliefs, in which those who live an enlightened life can escape the cycle of reincarnation. George also inserts the chant "Om" during the brief instrumental breaks.

In America, the single was mastered at a slightly faster speed than on the album version to "brighten" it for radio play.

"Give Me Love (Give Me Peace on Earth)" was George's second number one single in the U.S., knocking Paul's "My Love" out of the top spot. Ironically, George would be replaced at number one the following week by their fellow Apple artist Billy Preston via his hit "Will It Go Round in Circles". At one point, George, Paul and Preston held the first, second and third positions on the *Billboard* Hot 100.

George Harrison – vocals, guitars, slide guitar
Nicky Hopkins – piano
Gary Wright – organ
Klaus Voorman – bass
Jim Keltner – drums

24. LIVE AND LET DIE
Wings

Written by Paul and Linda McCartney
Recorded October 1972
Released June 1, 1973
Album: WINGSPAN

James Barry, who had written several James Bond movie scores, was unavailable during the production of 1973's *Live and Let Die*. When Beatles producer and arranger George Martin was commissioned to write the musical score, a Paul McCartney-penned theme song seemed like the perfect pairing.

After being sent a copy of the Ian Fleming novel the movie would be based upon, Paul read the book and wrote the theme in the same weekend. He recorded it with Wings shortly after, reuniting with his producer ally at Martin's AIR Studios in London. Three songs in one, "Live and Let Die" contains a piano ballad, a reggae-style break, and powerful orchestral interludes.

Since much of the movie takes place in New Orleans and the Caribbean, the producers felt it would be more appropriate for a black artist like Shirley Bassey or Thelma Houston to sing the theme. Paul decreed that he would only permit the song to be used if Wings' recording was used for the opening credits. That was agreed upon, and another version sung by B.J. Arnau appears elsewhere in the soundtrack.

Another #1 hit for Wings, "Live and Let Die" remains the most popular Bond theme and is a crowd favorite that has become a staple of Paul's concerts. The explosive instrumental break is always synchronized to equally bombastic pyrotechnics.

Paul McCartney – lead vocals, piano
Linda McCartney – backing vocals, keyboard
Henry McCullough – lead guitar
Denny Laine – backing vocals, bass
Denny Seiwell – drums
Ray Cooper – timpani, percussion

25. PHOTOGRAPH
Ringo Starr

Written by Richard Starkey and George Harrison
Recorded March 1973
Released September 24, 1973
Album: RINGO

Upon attending Mick Jagger's wedding in St. Tropez in May 1971, Ringo rented a luxury yacht and remained in the South of France for the Cannes Film Festival and the Monaco Grand Prix. George, a racing fan, joined him for the latter. The two began writing this bittersweet song about lost love while on the yacht.

During an onboard get-together, Ringo and George played "Photograph" for the other guests. Singer Cilla Black said she wanted to record the song as a single but was told by Starr that it was too good and he was keeping it for himself.

The version that appears on *Ringo* was recorded two years later utilizing much the same lineup of musicians as on George's *Living in the Material World* album. "Photograph" became Ringo's second #1 hit.

Ringo was Starr's most successful album and the first to contain contributions by all four ex-Beatles. The cover painting recalled the cover of *Sgt. Pepper's Lonely Hearts Club Band*, depicting an assortment of celebrities looking on. They include Peter Sellers, Harry Nilsson, Marc Bolan, Leon Russell, Yoko Ono, Linda McCartney, the Beatles, and the artist himself, Tim Bruckner.

Ringo Starr – vocals, drums
George Harrison – 12-string guitar, backing vocals
Vini Poncia – acoustic guitar, backing vocals
Jimmy Calvert – acoustic guitar
Nicky Hopkins – piano
Klaus Voorman – bass
Jim Keltner – drums
Bobby Keys – tenor saxophone
Lon Van Eaton, Derrek Van Eaton – percussion

26. HELEN WHEELS
Paul McCartney and Wings

Written by Paul and Linda McCartney
Recorded August 1973
Released October 26, 1973
Album: BAND ON THE RUN

"Helen Wheels" was the nickname Paul and Linda gave to their Land Rover, which they drove during their frequent road trips between Scotland and England. This freewheeling song chronicles the route by mapping the cities and towns along the way, namely Glasgow, Carlisle, Kendall, Liverpool, Birmingham, and London. Built around one chord with three very short visits to a second, the insistent forward motion effectively suggests the rhythm of the road.

The McCartneys wanted a change of venue in which to record "Helen Wheels" and the other new songs for their next album, *Band on the Run*. Since EMI had studios all over the world, Paul requested a list of their international locations. He decided on Lagos, Nigeria.

Weeks before they were to leave for Africa, guitarist Henry McCullough quit the band, citing musical differences. Hours before departure, drummer Denny Seiwell resigned as well. With Wings newly clipped, Paul, Linda and Denny Laine made the trip to Nigeria, along with their children, staff, and former Beatles engineer Geoff Emerick.

Lagos was hardly the tropical paradise they had hoped for. Arriving during monsoon season, they experienced frequent storms and outages. The studio itself was unfinished and rudimentary.

In the absence of McCullough and Seiwell, Paul intended to hire African musicians to supplement the Lagos sessions, but was met with resistance when the locals claimed he was trying to "steal" African music. So he, Linda and Denny Laine performed everything themselves. The result would be Wings' most acclaimed album.

Paul McCartney – lead vocals, guitar, bass, drums
Linda McCartney – backing vocals, keyboards
Denny Laine – backing vocals, guitar

27. MIND GAMES
John Lennon

Written by John Lennon
Recorded July 1973
Released October 29, 1973
Album: MIND GAMES

Originally written in 1969 and titled "Make Love, Not War", John felt that phrase had become a cliché and renamed it "Mind Games" after reading a book by human behavior researchers Robert Masters and Jean Houston. Their book, *Mind Games: The Guide to Inner Space*, promotes mind training with a goal of living with more focus and flexibility. Some of the authors' catch phrases appear in the song.

One lyric, "YES is the answer" harkens back to John's first encounter with Yoko Ono. In 1966, at a London gallery show of her avant-garde art, visitors were invited to climb a white ladder. Framed up on the ceiling in tiny letters—visible only through a supplied magnifying glass—was the word "YES". John resonated immediately with its positive message.

"Mind Games" was recorded at the beginning of a period that Lennon would call his Lost Weekend, which involved eighteen months of separation from Yoko. Frustrated and losing confidence in his songwriting abilities (his 1972 album *Some Time in New York City* was a critical and commercial letdown, particularly after 1971's *Imagine*), John and Yoko agreed that they needed some time apart. John moved in with their assistant May Pang with Yoko's blessing, feeling that Pang would look after John and keep him away from other women. For John, the summer of 1973 thru early 1975 became a period of drunken revelry, introspection, and a return to creative victory.

John Lennon – vocals, guitar, slide guitar, clavichord
David Spinozza – guitar
Gordon Edwards – bass
Jim Keltner – drums
Ken Ascher – Mellotron

28. YOU'RE SIXTEEN
Ringo Starr

Written by Robert B. Sherman and Richard M. Sherman
Recorded March 1973
Released December 3, 1973
Album: RINGO

Songwriting team Bob and Dick Sherman (aka the Sherman Brothers) were an award-winning fixture at Walt Disney Studios for five decades. They wrote many of the familiar Disney classics, from musicals such as *Mary Poppins* and *The Jungle Book* to "It's a Small World", which has played over 50 million times at the company's theme parks.

The Shermans enjoyed occasional pop music success, including "You're Sixteen", a 1960 hit recorded by Johnny Burnette. His version also appears prominently in the 1973 film *American Graffiti*, at a time when classic rock 'n' roll songs were coming back into vogue. "You're Sixteen" was chosen to be included on Ringo's self-titled album and became his third #1 single.

Recorded in Los Angeles, "You're Sixteen" featured Harry Nilsson multitracking all backing vocals. Some weeks later, Ringo went to London to record another song for his album with Paul McCartney. After hearing "You're Sixteen", Paul contributed to the instrumental break, doing his impression of a saxophone on kazoo. The result was labeled a "mouth sax solo." During the song's fadeout, a playful Ringo added bits of "I Don't Know Why I Love You (But I Do)" and "What Shall We Do with a Drunken Sailor".

Ringo Starr – vocals, drums
Nilsson – backing vocals
Paul McCartney – kazoo
Nicky Hopkins – piano
Vini Poncia – guitar
Jimmy Calvert – guitar
Klaus Voorman – bass
Jim Keltner – additional drums

29. MRS. VANDEBILT
Paul McCartney and Wings

Written by Paul and Linda McCartney
Recorded September 1973
Released January 1974
Album: BAND ON THE RUN

A catchphrase of English comedian and TV personality Charlie Chester was "Down in the jungle, living in a tent, better than a bungalow; no rent!" The McCartneys and Denny Laine felt some kinship with that sentiment while recording in Lagos, Nigeria, and incorporated a variation of Chester's saying into the opening verse of "Mrs. Vandebilt". The sound of laughter at the end of the song is another nod to the comedian.

Their Lagos experience, however, was no laughing matter. The first week they were there, while taking a stroll, Paul and Linda were robbed at knifepoint by a local gang. Along with Paul's watch, camera and cash, the robbers made away with his bag of demo tapes, lyrics and notes for all the songs to be recorded. Ironically, "Mrs. Vandebilt", which had been written beforehand, makes a reference to robbery. Adding insult to injury, the studio was hit with a power outage in the middle of recording the song.

The title is inspired by (and is a misspelling of) Gloria Vanderbilt, whose family made a fortune in the shipping industry during the 19th century. Their financial decline decades later is vaguely inferred in this song about carrying on in the face of misfortune. "Mrs. Vandebilt" was released as a single in Australia and other foreign territories.

Providing saxophone was Howie Casey, who had performed on the same Liverpool and Germany stages as the Beatles in 1960 with his rival group The Seniors.

Paul McCartney – vocals, bass, guitar, drums
Linda McCartney – electric piano, backing vocals
Denny Laine – guitar, backing vocals
Howie Casey – saxophone

30. JET
Paul McCartney and Wings

Written by Paul and Linda McCartney
Recorded September 1973
Released January 28, 1974
Album: BAND ON THE RUN

Paul has said that Jet was the name of a black Labrador puppy the couple had owned. In other interviews, he referred to a horse on their Scottish farm with that name. In any case, the dog and pony show that was their Nigerian fiasco saw Wings returning to London to finish their album in a proper studio.

"Jet" was the first order of business when they got back, and that session was not without its difficulties, either. While Paul and Denny were overdubbing instruments onto the basic track, engineer Geoff Emerick noticed that the "top end" (treble) was beginning to disappear, the result of a faulty reel of tape that was losing oxide with each new pass. Emerick hesitated to break the musicians' vibe by having them start over. Meanwhile, the audio continued to deteriorate. Fortunately, Paul ended the session before the tape completely wore out, and Emerick discreetly transferred everything to a fresh reel of tape. From there, everything went well, although Emerick spoke with mixed emotions about the basic tracks' "distinctively solid sound."

While the title of "Jet" (appropriate for a band called Wings) may have been inspired by an animal, the song itself is an exaggerated account of when the McCartneys announced to Linda's parents that they were going to get married. Linda's father, Lee Eastman, was not a "Sergeant Major," but Paul felt sufficiently intimidated by the prominent showbiz attorney. As for the "suffragette" mentioned in the song, that was nothing more than a convenient rhyme.

Paul McCartney – vocals, guitar, bass, drums
Linda McCartney – keyboards, Moog synthesizer, backing vocals
Denny Laine – guitar, backing vocals
Howie Casey – saxophone

31. OH MY MY
Ringo Starr

Written by Richard Starkey and Vini Poncia
Recorded March 1973
Released February 18, 1974
Album: RINGO

The dance craze of the 1970s was just finding its footing when Ringo released the third single from his self-titled album. Disco music as the world would come to know it was still some months away, but the four-on-the-floor thumping rhythm of "Oh My My" was a fitting foreshadow of things to come.

Its easy-to-move-to message that dancing is a prescription for the blues and has the healing power to "keep you alive" was written by Ringo and frequent co-writer Vini Poncia, who also penned the 1976 hit "You Make Me Feel Like Dancing" with Leo Sayer. Background singers include Martha Reeves of Martha & the Vandellas ("Dancing in the Streets", "Heat Wave").

Prior to 1974, Ringo had considered a movie career as a producer and actor, having already appeared in such films as *The Magic Christian, Blindman, Son of Dracula* and *Caveman*. However, the popularity of his *Ringo* album convinced him that music was still his primary calling. The album also goes down in history as the only solo release to include all four ex-Beatles, who each wrote and performed at least one song.

"Oh My My" was Ringo's fifth hit single as a solo artist. Because of its chart success, John Lennon sent Ringo a telegram saying, "Congratulations. How dare you? And please write me a hit song."

Ringo Starr – vocals, drums
Billy Preston – keyboards
Tom Scott – saxophone
Klaus Voorman – bass
Jim Keltner – additional drums
Martha Reeves – backing vocals
Merry Clayton – backing vocals

32. BAND ON THE RUN
Paul McCartney and Wings

Written by Paul and Linda McCartney
Recorded September 1973
Released January 28, 1974
Album: BAND ON THE RUN

During one of the Beatles' contentious meetings at Apple in 1969, George Harrison made the comment, "If I ever get out of this house." Paul adapted that line for "Band on the Run", a four-part medley depicting 1) being in prison, 2) planning an escape, 3) breaking out, and 4) running from the law. The medley approach recalled some of his previous hits (e.g. "Uncle Albert/Admiral Halsey" and "Live and Let Die") and utilized a 60-piece orchestra.

Along with symbolizing his breaking free from the Beatles, Paul has related the song to drug arrests of musicians, as well as the rigors of being on the road touring with a band.

The distinctive cover of the *Band on the Run* album depicts a prison break with Wings caught in a searchlight along with actors Christopher Lee and James Coburn, British celebrities Michael Parkinson, Kenny Lynch and Clement Freud, and boxer John Conteh. Photographer Clive Arrowsmith confessed to using the wrong film, which gave the photo shoot a yellowish hue, but Paul was pleased with the golden effect.

Prior to *Band on the Run*, Paul's solo singles had all been separate releases and not part of any album, a holdover practice from his years with the Beatles. He hadn't intended to release any of this album's songs as singles either, until prompted by a Capitol Records exec who convinced him they would take the album to the top, which they did. *Band on the Run* achieved triple platinum status, selling over six million copies, making it the most successful of all post-Beatles solo albums.

Paul McCartney – vocals, guitars, synthesizer, bass, drums
Linda McCartney – backing vocals, keyboards
Denny Laine – backing vocals, guitar, slide guitar

33. WHATEVER GETS YOU THROUGH THE NIGHT
John Lennon

Written by John Lennon
Recorded June 1974
Released September 23, 1974
Album: WALLS AND BRIDGES

Channel surfing one night, John came upon TV preacher Reverend Ike. During that particular sermon, the evangelist said, "It's whatever gets you through the night." John loved the line and developed lyrics based on it.

Musically, he found inspiration in George McRae's 1974 hit "Rock Your Baby" (written by K.C. of Sunshine Band fame), although the finished product bears little resemblance to disco.

During the recording session, Elton John visited the studio and asked if he could play piano. As the song took shape, Elton would also play organ and sing harmony throughout.

Elton felt the song would be a #1 hit, but John didn't believe it was strong enough. Elton made a bet that if it did reach the top of the charts, John would have to perform on stage with him.

The raucous superstar duet "Whatever Gets You Through the Night" did become John's first #1 solo single in America. Two weeks later he played with Elton at Madison Square Garden in what would be his last public performance.

Backstage, via some intervention from Paul, John reunited with Yoko.

John Lennon – vocals, guitar
Elton John – vocals, piano, organ
Bobby Keys – tenor saxophone
Ron Aprea – alto saxophone
Jesse Ed Davis – electric guitar
Eddie Mottau – acoustic guitar
Ken Ascher – clavinet
Klaus Voorman – bass
Jim Keltner – drums
Arthur Jenkins – percussion

34. WALKING IN THE PARK WITH ELOISE
The Country Hams (Wings)

Written by James McCartney
Recorded July 1974
Released October 18, 1974
Album: WINGS AT THE SPEED OF SOUND

Following the success of "Band on the Run", Paul prepared for an American tour by hiring two new musicians to replace the departed Seiwell and McCullough. Drummer Geoff Britton, formerly of the progressive rock band East of Eden, and Jimmy McCulloch, lead guitarist of Thunderclap Newman ("Something in the Air") joined the McCartneys for seven weeks of rehearsal at a Nashville farm.

Though their stay had been intended purely for rehearsal, Paul rented a local studio for the final two weeks and recorded several songs, including an instrumental his father Jim had written many years prior, "Walking in the Park with Eloise". As a tribute to the man who had introduced Paul to the many styles of music he grew to love and be inspired by, he recruited Nashville cats Floyd Cramer and Chet Atkins to join in along with a Dixieland horn section.

Released as a single under the pseudonym The Country Hams, "Walking in the Park with Eloise" later became a bonus track on *Wings at the Speed of Sound*. In a 1982 interview, Paul chose it as one of eight songs he would take with him if he were stranded on a desert island, right alongside Elvis' "Heartbreak Hotel", Chuck Berry's "Sweet Little Sixteen", Little Richard's "Tutti Frutti" and other formative songs from his youth. He also chose John Lennon's "Beautiful Boy".

Paul McCartney – bass, washboard
Linda McCartney – keyboards
Denny Laine – guitar
Jimmy McCulloch – acoustic guitar
Geoff Britton – drums
Chet Atkins – guitar
Floyd Cramer – piano

35. JUNIOR'S FARM
Paul McCartney and Wings

Written by Paul and Linda McCartney
Recorded July 16-18, 1974
Released October 25, 1974
Album: VENUS AND MARS

Paul's rehearsal space with his new 1974 band lineup was a farm near Lebanon, Tennessee, owned by country songwriter Curly Putman, Jr., whose credits include "D-I-V-O-R-C-E". While there, Paul wrote this rocker in honor of his host.

"Junior's Farm", the last song they recorded while in Nashville, is a collection of fictional scenes involving gamblers, Eskimos, sea lions, Parliament, Richard Nixon, and Oliver Hardy. But the chorus does speak of going to Junior's farm where they could "lay low." Indeed, Wings had hoped that their pre-tour hideaway would be unpublicized, but once word got out that the McCartneys were in town, the studio was surrounded by fans each night they recorded.

Ernie Winfrey, Sound Shop engineer at the time, recalls that Paul only had a visitor's visa and was not authorized to work in the U.S., so their sessions were kept under wraps as much as possible. Winfrey adds that guitarist Jimmy McCulloch caused some friction, showing up drunk and throwing a bottle at the control room window. After being banished from the studio, his rowdy behavior ran him afoul of the local law. Only through having friends in high places did he escape jail time.

Aside from McCulloch's hijinx and toddler Stella's running through a glass door—requiring a trip to the E.R.—Paul and Linda enjoyed their time in Music City, visiting drive-in theaters, dining at the Loveless Café, and seeing Dolly Parton in concert.

Paul McCartney – vocals, bass
Linda McCartney – keyboards, backing vocals
Denny Laine – guitars, backing vocals
Jimmy McCulloch – lead guitar, backing vocals
Geoff Britton – drums

36. ONLY YOU
Ringo Starr

Written by Samuel "Buck" Ram
Recorded August 6, 1974
Released November 15, 1974
Album: GOODNIGHT VIENNA

One of the most successful songwriters of the 20th century, Buck Ram produced and penned hits for many artists during the '50s, including the Coasters, the Penguins, the Drifters, and the Platters, whose first hit in the summer of 1955 was "Only You (And You Alone)". At the suggestion of John Lennon, Ringo recorded this remake nineteen years later.

Prompted by the popularity of his previous album, Ringo recruited basically the same musicians for his fourth collection, *Goodnight Vienna*. Additional contributors this time around were Elton John, Robbie Robertson of The Band, Dr. John ("Right Place Wrong Time") and Lennon cohort May Pang.

Ringo's rendition of "Only You" departed from the 12/8 tempo of The Platters' classic. His relaxed 4/4 interpretation was driven by an acoustic guitar played by John, who also recorded a guide vocal while in the studio. John's version, using the same tracks but with a more electric-sounding mix, appeared on 1998's *John Lennon Anthology* boxed set.

Featuring background vocals by Harry Nilsson, "Only You" was the first single released from *Goodnight Vienna* and became Ringo's sixth consecutive top ten hit.

Ringo Starr – vocals, drums
John Lennon – acoustic guitar
Harry Nilsson – backing vocals
Jesse Ed Davis – electric guitar
Steve Cropper – electric guitar
Billy Preston – electric piano
Klaus Voorman – bass
Jim Keltner – additional drums

37. DARK HORSE
George Harrison

Written by George Harrison
Recorded October 30, 1974
Released November 18, 1974
Album: DARK HORSE

The term "dark horse" refers to an underdog competitor who scores an unexpected victory. Music critics had considered George a dark horse, having been The Quiet Beatle who made good.

George was unaware of that definition when he wrote the title song and only single from his next album. He thought a dark horse was a rebel, something he considered himself to be during 1973-74. George's "naughty period," as he called it, was in response to criticism over the spiritual overtones of his two previous albums and his preoccupation with the Hare Krishna movement. His quest for enlightenment became, for the time, one of self-indulgence.

George's drinking, drugging and dalliances led to his wife Pattie leaving him for rocker Ron Wood (she would later marry George's friend Eric Clapton, who had been wooing her since 1970). The woman who had once inspired "Something" was now at the center of George's single "Dark Horse" as well as other contentious tunes in which he seems to fault himself as well.

George Harrison – vocals, guitar
Billy Preston – electric piano
Robben Ford – acoustic guitar
Willie Weeks – bass
Jim Keltner – drums
Andy Newark – drums
Tom Scott – flute
Jim Horn – flute
Chuck Findley – flute
Emil Richards – percussion
Derrek Van Eaton – backing vocals
Lon Van Eaton – backing vocals

38. DING DONG, DING DONG
George Harrison

Written by George Harrison
Recorded November 1973 and October 1974
Released December 6, 1974
Album: DARK HORSE

Hoping to create a new pop standard for the holidays, George recorded the rhythm tracks for "Ding Dong, Ding Dong" in late 1973 at his 16-track home studio at Friar Park, a sprawling neo-gothic estate in Henley-on-Thames, England, which he had purchased in 1970.

The mansion and grounds were the former home of 19th Century baron and lawyer Sir Frankie Crisp, who left a legacy all around the estate via engraved quotes. George incorporated a number of these inspirational phrases in the verses of "Ding Dong", while the main chorus, a repetition of "Ring out the old, ring in the new, ring out the false, ring in the true" is attributed to poet Lord Tennyson.

George emulated Phil Spector's wall of sound with a massive arrangement that included then-Faces guitarist Ron Wood. By the time the album came out, Wood was courting George's wife Pattie. Wood is credited on *Dark Horse* as "Ron Would if you let him".

The final overdubs for "Ding Dong" were completed hastily before George was to embark on a November 1974 tour. His raspy vocal foretold laryngitis, which would haunt his live concerts.

George Harrison – vocals, guitars, organ, clavinet, percussion
Gary Wright – piano
Ron Wood – electric guitar
Alvin Lee – electric guitar
Mick Jones – acoustic guitar
Tom Scott – tenor sax, baritone sax
Klaus Voorman – bass
Ringo Starr – drums
Jim Keltner – additional drums
Uncredited – female backing singers

39. #9 DREAM
John Lennon

Written by John Lennon
Recorded July 23, 1974
Released December 16, 1974
Album: WALLS AND BRIDGES

As the title suggests, "#9 Dream" had its origins when both a melody and the phrase "Ah! böwakawa poussé, poussé" came to John in his sleep. He wrote it down immediately upon awakening. The words are meaningless, but John liked the sound of them and attempted to recreate the vibe of his vision in this, his second single from *Walls and Bridges*.

John's original title for "#9 Dream" was "So Long Ago". Considering the song to be a gift, he changed the name in honor of the number that he felt followed him in pivotal ways throughout his life: He was born on the ninth day of the month; he lived at 9 Newcastle Road; the Beatles were first seen by manager Brian Epstein on November 9, 1961; John left the Beatles in 1969 after nine years, and so on.

The string arrangement of "#9 Dream" intentionally resembled Harry Nilsson's "Many Rivers to Cross", which John produced earlier that year.

During the song, John's name is whispered, heard backwards the second time around. According to May Pang, the session vocalist originally hired to speak that part didn't show up, so she filled in.

John Lennon – vocals, acoustic guitar
Jesse Ed Davis – guitar
Eddie Mottau – acoustic guitar
Nicky Hopkins – electric piano
Ken Ascher – clavinet
Bobby Keys – saxophone
Klaus Voorman – bass
Jim Keltner – drums
Arthur Jenkins – percussion

40. NO NO SONG
Ringo Starr

Written by Hoyt Axton and David Jackson
Recorded July 1974
Released January 27, 1975
Album: GOODNIGHT VIENNA

Country singer Hoyt Axton (writer of the Three Dog Night hit "Joy to the World") was no stranger to cocaine addiction. He teamed up with bassist and comedian David Jackson to write this tongue-in-cheek anti-drug song to mock his personal struggle. In "No No Song", the singer is offered marijuana from Colombia, cocaine from Spain, and moonshine from Nashville, but turns them all down.

Ringo's version is performed with a festive South American feel. The melody of the instrumental break bears such a strong resemblance to a Rhodesian song called "Skokiaan" (recorded in the '50s by Mambo king Perez Prado) that the most recent rereleases of Ringo's hit are entitled "No No Song/Skokiaan".

Fairly difficult to distinguish over the music, Ringo interjects some spoken lines. In the Nashville section, after being offered whiskey said to be the "best in all the land," Ringo shouts, "And he wasn't joking!" During the fadeout, he and Nilsson ask the barman for another drink.

Coerced by his producer, Ringo did not initially want to record what would become one of his most popular hits. At the time of recording "No No Song", he himself was overindulging in the very things the song professes to resist and had no intention of quitting.

He did clean up years later after entering rehab. He has since introduced this song in concert as the one that "saved me".

Ringo Starr – vocals, drums, percussion
Harry Nilsson – backup vocals
Nicky Hopkins – electric piano
Jesse Ed Davis – guitar
Klaus Voorman – bass
Trevor Lawrence, Bobby Keyes – horns

41. SNOOKEROO
Ringo Starr

Written by Elton John and Bernie Taupin
Recorded July 1974
Released February 21, 1975
Album: GOODNIGHT VIENNA

Riding high on his own success in the early '70s and already having recorded with John Lennon, Elton John wrote this song specifically with Ringo in mind. While the song identifies its hero as being from a working town in northern England (which Ringo was), it alludes to being born on the eve of Halloween (which Ringo wasn't).

The semi-fictitious lyrics portray its singer as a carefree gadabout with a penchant for snooker, a British version of pool. Mentioned are a drunk father and a wayward sister. Ringo has no sister but did have a father who drank and left the family early on. Unmentioned was the biggest trial of Ringo's childhood, his serious health problems. He spent a total of three years in hospitals for peritonitis and tuberculosis. His illnesses were so critical that his mother Elsie was told on at least three occasions that he could die.

The lyrics of "Snookeroo" also mention having his childhood home torn down by a wrecking ball. In a strange twist of fate, Ringo's birthplace in Dingle, Liverpool was indeed threatened with demolition thirty years after this song as part of a controversial housing renewal project. Following a seven-year battle, hundreds of homes were taken down, but Ringo's house at 9 Madryn Street was among those spared.

Ringo Starr – vocals, drums
Elton John – piano
Robbie Robertson – guitar
James Newton Howard – synthesizer
Klaus Voorman – bass
Jim Keltner – drums
Trevor Lawrence, Steve Madaio, Chuck Findley – horns
Clydie King, Linda Lawrence, Joe Greene – backing vocals

42. STAND BY ME
John Lennon

Written by Ben E. King, Jerry Leiber and Mike Stoller
Recorded October 21, 1974
Released March 10, 1975
Album: ROCK 'N' ROLL

The opening lyrics of the Beatles' 1969 hit "Come Together" and the melody that accompanies it were so similar to Chuck Berry's 1956 car song "You Can't Catch Me" that Big Seven Publishing, owned by Morris Levy, proceeded to sue John for copyright infringement.

In October 1973 the case was settled out of court with the condition that John would record three Big Seven songs on his next release. Studio sessions for John's album *Rock 'n' Roll* began almost immediately under the direction of Phil Spector. But, when the quirky producer became unreachable for several months and then was in a coma following a car accident, the project was put aside.

Consequently, *Walls and Bridges* was released instead of *Rock 'n' Roll*, and Levy threatened another lawsuit. To assure Levy that the album would happen, John sent him rough, unfinished mixes. Levy released the songs as is on his own label, and John ended up suing *him* (being awarded $142,700). The official album was eventually released by John and included "You Can't Catch Me".

"Stand by Me" was the only American single from *Rock 'n' Roll*. It became John's last album until he recorded again in 1980. With no contractual obligations, he took a five-year break to be a house husband and raise his baby boy Sean, born on John's 35th birthday.

John Lennon – vocals, acoustic guitar
Eddie Montau, Jesse Ed Davis, Peter Jameson – guitars
Ken Ascher – piano
Joseph Temperley, Frank Vicari, Dennis Morouse – saxophones
Klaus Voorman – bass
Jim Keltner – drums
Arthur Jenkins – percussion

43. LISTEN TO WHAT THE MAN SAID
Wings

Written by Paul and Linda McCartney
Recorded January 31, 1975
Released May 16, 1975
Album: VENUS AND MARS

In late 1974, sessions began in London for Wings' new album, *Venus and Mars*. Three songs in, drummer Geoff Britton quit the band after personality clashes with Denny and Jimmy. Jazz drummer Joe English soon rounded out the next incarnation of Wings.

Paul decided to complete *Venus and Mars* in New Orleans for both inspiration and tax-avoidance reasons. The colorful party atmosphere and mix of cultures the French Quarter is known for felt like the ideal place to let the good times roll.

"Listen to What the Man Said" was a song that Paul said people especially enjoyed whenever he played it for them on the piano. Once in the studio, he wasn't satisfied with the result. Even the participation of Traffic guitarist Dave Mason wasn't enough to give the track the drive Paul had envisioned. During wrap-up sessions in L.A., someone mentioned that acclaimed saxophonist Tom Scott lived nearby. Upon arriving, Scott listened to the track and adlibbed a solo that was so on the money that his first take was the one used.

The song opens with Paul's deep-throated imitation of Leo Nocentelli, a New Orleans guitarist who appears elsewhere on *Venus and Mars*: "All right, OK, very good to see you down in New Orleans, man; yeah, yeah, reet, yeah, yeah." ("Reet" is slang for "very good".)

Paul McCartney – vocals, bass, keyboards, percussion
Linda McCartney – keyboards, backing vocals, percussion
Denny Laine – guitars, backing vocals, percussion
Jimmy McCulloch – guitars
Dave Mason – guitars
Joe English – drums
Tom Scott – soprano saxophone

44. GOODNIGHT VIENNA
Ringo Starr

Written by John Lennon
Recorded August 1974
Released June 2, 1975
Album: GOODNIGHT VIENNA

The British phrase "Goodnight Vienna" has origins in a romantic 1932 musical in which lovers are separated by war. It has come to mean "it's all over."

Written by John during his 18-month separation from Yoko, the upbeat song about a partygoer with paranoia comes with a certain irony. His "Lost Weekend" was filled with headline-making madness just as excessive as the wild soiree spelled out in the song.

The album cover of *Goodnight Vienna* depicts Ringo boarding a flying saucer and dressed as Klaatu from the classic sci-fi film *The Day the Earth Stood Still*. In the movie, Klaatu warned Earth that humanity must learn to live in peace.

Ringo's album cover would play an unwitting role in 1976 rumors that the Beatles had reunited when an album with distinctly Beatlesque overtones was released under the pseudonym Klaatu. The lack of photos, bios or musician credits on the album fueled speculation on a par with the "Paul is dead" hoax of 1966. Klaatu turned out to be an obscure Canadian band that happily rode the wave of publicity.

Ringo Starr – vocals, drums
John Lennon – vocals, piano
Billy Preston – clavinet
Lon Van Eaton, Jesse Ed Davis – guitars
Carl Fortina – accordion
Klaus Voorman – bass
Jim Keltner – drums
Bobby Keys, Trevor Lawrence, Steve Madaio, Lon Can Eaton – horns
Clydie King, The Blackberries, The Masst Abbots – backing vocals

45. YA YA
John Lennon

Written by Lee Dorsey, Clarence Lewis, Morgan Robinson
Recorded July–August 1974
Released June 1975
Album: ROCK 'N' ROLL

While performing in Hamburg and Liverpool in their early days, the Beatles got their hands on as many American pop and R&B records as they could in order to stay on top of what the crowds wanted. Part of their stage repertoire was "Ya Ya", a top ten hit by Lee Dorsey in 1961.

Dorsey, a lightweight boxer who competed under the name Kid Chocolate, retired at age 31 and began singing in nightclubs. A few unsuccessful singles later, he co-wrote and recorded "Ya Ya", inspired by a children's jump roping chant. It was Dorsey's biggest hit next to "Working in the Coal Mine" in 1966.

As part of John's copyright settlement with Morris Levy's publishing company over "Come Together", he returned to his roots with a cover of "Ya Ya" on his album *Rock 'n' Roll*. The joyful remake was released as a single in Germany, where the song had been a particular favorite of the Beatles' first followers.

The closing song on John's previous album, *Walls and Bridges*, was a short excerpt of a different recording of "Ya Ya", performed with John on piano and his visiting 11-year-old son Julian on drums. Their four-on-the-floor rendition was reminiscent of the Beatles' "Why Don't We Do It in the Road."

John Lennon – vocals, electric guitar
Jessie Ed Davis – electric guitar
Eddie Mottau – acoustic guitar
Ken Ascher – piano
Klaus Voorman – bass
Joseph Temperley, Frank Vicari, Dennis Morouse – saxophones
Jim Keltner – drums
Arthur Jenkins – percussion

46. YOU
George Harrison

Written by George Harrison
Recorded February 1971 and May 1975
Released September 12, 1975
Album: EXTRA TEXTURE (READ ALL ABOUT IT)

The Beatles first became connected to Phil Spector in 1969 when the well-known producer was hired to oversee their album *Let It Be*. Later collaborations with John and George led to his appointment as A&R Director at Apple Records. In this role, he insisted that his wife Ronnie ("Be My Baby") record an album on the label. George wrote "You" with her in mind, seeking a classic Ronettes feel.

The backing track was recorded in 1971 during sessions for *All Things Must Pass*. Although it was intended to be Ronnie Spector's comeback single, it was never released.

George forgot all about the song until 1975 while working on his album *Extra Texture*. He resurrected the track and put his own vocals on it, but the music was recorded in a key more suitable for Ronnie Spector. He struggled to reach the high notes until tape speed manipulation came to the rescue. Ronnie Spector's voice from her original recording can sometimes be heard in the background.

"You" was the opening song on *Extra Texture*, the last album any Beatle would record on their Apple label. From this point on, George would be releasing under his own label, Dark Horse Records.

George Harrison – vocals, guitars
Ronnie Spector – vocals
Leon Russell – piano
Gary Wright – electric piano
David Foster – organ, synthesizer
Jim Horn – saxophone
Carl Radle – bass
Jim Keltner – drums
Jim Gordon – drums, percussion

47. LETTING GO
Wings

Written by Paul and Linda McCartney
Recorded November 1974
Released October 4, 1975
Album: VENUS AND MARS

One of the few songs recorded before drummer Geoff Britton left the band, "Letting Go" is a love song of a different type. In this power ballad of infatuation, the singer praises his woman and wants the world to know how incredible she is. He is overwhelmed by her to the point of surrendering to her power.

The line "Like a lucifer she'll always shine" isn't inferring that she's a devil woman. In British parlance, a lucifer is the type of match that can be struck on any surface (as opposed to a safety match, requiring the side of a matchbox).

Paul had been instrumental in John Lennon's reconciliation with Yoko, which occurred shortly before Paul began work on *Venus and Mars*. Upon hearing that Paul would be coming to America to record his latest album, John had intended to meet Paul during those sessions in New Orleans and possibly do some collaboration again. According to May Pang, the closer the time came, the more enthusiastically John spoke about it.

However, the reunion that the music world was waiting for never happened because John had moved back home with Yoko, whose hold on him was said to be so strong that he felt unable to leave her side.

Paul McCartney – vocals, bass, keyboards
Linda McCartney – backing vocals, organ
Jimmy McCulloch – electric guitar
Geoff Britton – drums
Denny Laine – backing vocals
Clyde Kerr – trumpet
John Longo – trumpet
Michael Pierce, Alvin Thomas, Carl Blouin – saxophones

48. VENUS AND MARS/ROCK SHOW
Wings

Written by Paul and Linda McCartney
Recorded January 16, 1975
Released October 27, 1975
Album: VENUS AND MARS

The two-song medley that opens *Venus and Mars* also opened the Wings Over the World Tour during 1975-76. Its spacey and slightly mysterious introduction builds ample anticipation for the "rock show" it bursts into.

Against the unlikely pairing of an acoustic guitar and a Moog synthesizer, the "Venus and Mars" portion depicts sitting in an arena before a concert, entranced by stage lights and sipping strawberry wine with a friend who likes astrology. When Paul wrote the song, he hadn't considered that Venus and Mars conveniently happen to be the two closest planets to Earth, but merely chose two celestial bodies that sounded good together.

Some assumed "Mars" was meant to be Paul and that "Venus" was Linda. Paul dismissed all such suggestions. (John Gray's *Men are from Mars, Women are from Venus* didn't come out until 1992.)

The harder "Rock Song" that follows mentions Led Zeppelin's Jimmy Page and characters named Silly Willy and Mademoiselle Kitty. Also specified are concert venues Paul has played. One line speaks of the sound being "louder at the Rainbow." London's Rainbow Theater was the site of a 1972 Deep Purple concert where the volume reached a deafening 117 decibels that allegedly knocked fans unconscious.

Paul McCartney – vocals, bass, guitar, keyboards, Mellotron, finger cymbals, hand bells
Linda McCartney – backing vocals, piano, organ, synthesizer, hand bells
Denny Laine – backing vocals, guitar, sitar, synthesizer, hand bells
Jimmy McCulloch – guitars, synthesizer, hand bells
Joe English – drums

49. THIS GUITAR (CAN'T KEEP FROM CRYING)
George Harrison

Written by George Harrison
Recorded April 1975
Released December 8, 1975
Album: EXTRA TEXTURE (READ ALL ABOUT IT)

George's 1974 "Dark Horse" tour was the first series of American concert dates by a Beatle since their 1966 concert in Candlestick Park, San Francisco. Fans hoping to relive the glory days of Beatlemania (and perhaps a surprise reunion on stage) were disappointed by the emphasis on unfamiliar songs, spiritual banter, Ravi Shankar's Indian music, and an ex-Beatle whose voice was rough from laryngitis. George's tour was mocked in some print reviews as the "Dark Hoarse" tour.

In particular, criticism fired off by the traditionally supportive *Rolling Stone* branded George's efforts nothing short of a calamity. The music magazine's reviews deprecating the tour were especially hurtful to George, who would not tour again until 1991.

"This Guitar (Can't Keep from Crying)" is in direct response to the negativity George had received for his tour and for the direction of his music in the mid-'70s. Bearing a structural resemblance to his acclaimed White Album song "While My Guitar Gently Weeps", this bitter follow-up speaks of hate and ignorance and climbing "Rolling Stone walls."

Klaus Voorman, the bassist who had been a fixture at George, John and Ringo sessions, found the studio atmosphere so depressing and unhealthy during sessions for *Extra Texture* that he chose not to participate during much of it. For this song, George played the bass part on a synthesizer.

George Harrison – vocals, 12-string guitar, slide guitar, ARP bass
Jesse Ed Davis – electric guitar
David Foster – piano
Gary Wright – ARP strings
Jim Keltner – drums

50. SILLY LOVE SONGS
Wings

Written by Paul and Linda McCartney
Recorded January 16, 1976
Released April 1, 1976
Album: WINGS AT THE SPEED OF SOUND

When John Lennon claimed in an interview that Paul only writes "silly love songs," he could not have imagined that he would help inspire Wings' most successful solo single. Paul's musical retort to John and any other critic who felt the same way was a joyful tribute to the very thing he was criticized for.

And listeners loved it. "Silly Love Songs" spent five weeks at #1 and quickly sold over a million copies. This first hit single from *Wings at the Speed of Sound* dutifully defended Paul's penchant for writing inoffensive pop that's easy to swallow and easy to dance to.

Written while on vacation in Hawaii and recorded at Abbey Road Studios, the song starts with simple piano chords in sync with a loop of factory sounds. Once drums and an intricate bass line kick in, it builds to a lengthy climax in which Paul, Linda and Denny reprise different parts of the song in melodic counterpoint with each other. Shortly before Denny sings, he says, "Latin," a reference to the percussion he also contributes during that section.

Paul's fifth solo album reflected a further response to critics who regarded Wings as merely Paul's backup band. *Wings at the Speed of Sound* saw each member of the group singing lead vocal on at least one song.

Paul McCartney – lead vocals, bass
Linda McCartney – backing vocals, piano
Denny Laine – backing vocals, percussion
Joe English – drums
Tony Dorsey – trombone
Steve Howard – trumpet
Thaddeus Richard – saxophone
Howie Casey – saxophone

51. LET 'EM IN
Wings

Written by Paul and Linda McCartney
Recorded February 4, 1976
Released July 23, 1976
Album: WINGS AT THE SPEED OF SOUND

When Paul began writing "Let 'Em In", he had in mind to give it to Ringo, but soon decided it would be better suited to Wings. In the song, he "opens the door" to welcome a variety of visitors, populating the lyrics with people from his own life and times.

Paul name-drops the people dropping in either literally or via a pseudonym: "Sister Suzy" (Linda's Jamaican nickname), "brother John" (Linda's brother John Eastman, although Paul has been equally content with its popular interpretation as meaning John Lennon), "Martin Luther" (King, the fallen minister), "Phil and Don" (sung in harmony as befitting the Everly Brothers), "brother Michael" (Paul's brother, musician Mike McGear), "Uncle Ernie" (Ringo, recalling his role in the 1972 remake of *Tommy*), and "Auntie Jin" (Paul's nickname for his aunt Jane McCartney Harris). In the final go-round of shout-outs he substitutes "Uncle Ian" (Ian Harris).

The Westminster chimes doorbell that opens the song was suggested by drummer Joe English. Continuing in the spirit of special effects, the lengthy sound of a creaking door precedes the military beat of a fife and drum corps, signifying the parade of visitors coming in.

Paul McCartney – lead vocals, piano
Linda McCartney – backing vocals
Denny Laine – backing vocals, military drums
Jimmy McCulloch – bass
Joe English – drums
Tony Dorsey – trombone
Steve Howard – trumpet, flute
Thaddeus Richard – saxophone
Howie Casey – saxophone

52. A DOSE OF ROCK 'N' ROLL
Ringo

Written by Carl Groszman
Recorded April 1976
Released September 20, 1976
Album: RINGO'S ROTOGRAVURE

By 1976, all of the former Beatles had moved on from Apple Records and either negotiated deals with other record companies or created their own. Ringo's well-intentioned but ill-fated venture, Ring O' Records, is a label he never recorded for but which was designed—much like Apple had been—to promote struggling artists. Ring O' Records (a name suggested by John Lennon) signed eleven acts and released five albums, most of those only in Europe.

One of the artists signed to Ringo's label was Australian songwriter and guitarist Carl Groszman. Choosing songs for his own next album, Ringo came across Groszman's "A Dose of Rock 'n' Roll" and it became the first single from his *Ringo's Rotogravure* LP on Atlantic Records.

Ringo's vocal begins accompanied by unison guitar played by Peter Frampton, using the "talk-box" human voice emulator famously heard on his 1976 hits "Do You Feel Like I Do" and "Show Me the Way". Frampton was first introduced to the effect via guitarist Pete Drake while visiting a session for George's *All Things Must Pass* album.

Model and rock photographer Nancy Andrews—Ringo's girlfriend at the time—named her 2008 biography after this song.

Ringo Starr – vocals, drums
Peter Frampton, Danny Kortchmar, Jesse Ed Davis – guitars
Dr. John – keyboards
Klaus Voorman – bass
Randy Brecker, Alan Rubin – trumpets
Michael Brecker, George Young, Lewis Delgatto – saxophones
Melissa Manchester, Duitch Helmer, Joe Bean, Vini Poncia –
    backing vocals

53. YOU DON'T KNOW ME AT ALL
Ringo Starr

Written by Dave Jordan
Recorded April 1976
Released October 15, 1976
Album: RINGO'S ROTOGRAVURE

Nancy Lee Andrews already knew George Harrison and John Lennon through her boyfriend, Carl Radle, a session musician who played bass on *All Things Must Pass* and *The Concert for Bangladesh*. In the spring of 1974, she attended a birthday party at John's Santa Monica house for former Beatles roadie Mal Evans. Invited to join in a poker game, she found herself sitting next to Ringo. The two clicked and they dated for six years.

Ringo admitted to Nancy early on that he had manic-depressive tendencies. Estrangement from his first wife Maureen, coupled with his impulse to imbibe, didn't help his mood swings. Behind the scenes, the real Richard Starkey wasn't the happy-go-lucky Ringo known to his fans. In one episode of drunken desperation, he completely shaved his head and eyebrows. "It was a time when you either cut your wrists or your hair," he explained in a *People* interview, "and I'm a coward."

Ringo seemed to enjoy showing off his shockingly different visage in the music video for his next single, "You Don't Know Me at All". Released in Europe, the song was written by Dave Jordan, a New Zealand songwriter who moved to London in the '70s to try his luck there. The upbeat love song recalls the message of Eddy Arnold's similarly titled "You Don't Know Me", confessing to an unspoken devotion.

Ringo Starr – vocals, drums
Lon Van Eaton – guitar
John Jarvis – piano
Cooker Lo Presti – bass
Jim Keltner – drums
Duitch Helmer, Vini Poncia – backing vocals

54. LAS BRISAS
Ringo Starr

Written by Richard Starkey and Nancy Andrews
Recorded April 1976
Released September 20, 1976
Album: RINGO'S ROTOGRAVURE

Ringo has vacationed in Central America numerous times. When EMI/Capitol Records opened new offices in Mexico, he was invited to help inaugurate it. While there, he stayed at the Hotel Las Brisas in Acapulco. He enjoyed his time at the luxury resort and was only too happy to return in 1974 during his promotional tour for *Goodnight Vienna*. This time girlfriend Nancy Andrews joined him.

Taken with the romantic language of Mexico, Nancy learned a little Spanish, specifically the hotel's namesake, *las brisas* ("the breeze"), and *penumbra* ("sunset"), both of which she incorporated into a poem. When Ringo realized she was writing an ode to their seaside getaway, he decided they should turn it into a song. "Las Brisas" was released as a single only in South America.

To perform the song, Ringo wanted an authentic Mariachi band. Back in L.A., he scouted Mexican restaurants until he found Los Galleros, who had never been in a recording studio before and didn't speak English. According to Ringo, the band was tuning up their instruments when he arrived for the session. Once they recognized him, they all attempted to say "Beatles" but couldn't pronounce it correctly. Their attempts of "Bottles" and "Bettles" had everyone erupting in laughter.

This wasn't the only time Ringo commissioned a Mariachi band. For John Lennon's birthday in 1974, he hired one in New York to serenade John outside the Dakota. That plan failed when the leader of the group got mugged the night before and the band never showed up.

Ringo Starr – vocals, maracas
Los Galleros – guitar, bass, violins, trumpets
Vini Poncia – backing vocals

55. THIS SONG
George Harrison

Written by George Harrison
Recorded May–September 1976
Released November 15, 1976
Album: THIRTY THREE & 1/3

George met Eric Idle at a 1975 screening of *Monty Python and the Holy Grail* in Los Angeles. They quickly became good friends, finding common ground in parody and a sarcastic sense of humor. Indeed, George would need some cheering up in 1976 after losing his court battle to Bright Tunes in the copyright infringement suit involving "My Sweet Lord" and the Chiffons' "He's So Fine".

During the long legal ordeal, during which both songs were torturously analyzed and compared, George became disillusioned as a songwriter, saying that every time he turned on the radio he would hear songs that sounded like other songs. But, as John, Paul, and he himself had done before, George took a bad situation and wrote a hit single in response. A week after the ruling, he came up with "This Song", a taunting tune that had "nothing *Bright* about it."

To help promote the single, George created a zany Monty Python-style music video. Filmed on a Sunday in an L.A. courtroom, the mock plagiarism trial included Ron Wood as an old lady, George's future wife Olivia Arias as Lady Justice, and drummer Jim Keltner as the judge, keeping time with his gavel.

The title of George's new album, *Thirty Three & 1/3,* was not just the speed the LP played at, but George's age at the time of its release.

George Harrison – vocals, guitars, tambourine
Billy Preston – organ
Richard Tee – piano
Tom Scott – saxophone
Willie Weeks – bass
Alvin Taylor – drums
Eric Idle – dialogue

56. CRACKERBOX PALACE
George Harrison

Written by George Harrison
Recorded May–September 1976
Released January 24, 1977
Album: THIRTY THREE & 1/3

Richard "Lord" Buckley was an American comedian and recording artist popular in the '50s for his eccentric aristocratic presence. Bob Dylan, Arlo Guthrie, and Frank Zappa all were influenced by the hipster's dry wit, as was George. In 1975, George had the opportunity to visit the late comedian's home in Los Angeles, which Buckley called "Crackerbox Palace." George liked that nickname so much that it became the moniker for his own 30-room mansion, Friar Park, and the inspiration for his next single from *Thirty Three & 1/3*.

The whimsical song suggests that life is a "Crackerbox Palace" of good and bad, of love and conformity. Lyrics include references to Lord Buckley ("the Lord is well and inside of you") and the comedian's manager, George Greif. A fan of Mel Brooks films as well, George says, "It's twue, it's twue" (as spoken by Madeline Kahn in *Blazing Saddles)* during the instrumental break.

Eric Idle directed a music video of "Crackerbox Palace" for *Saturday Night Live*, filmed inside the mansion and on the grounds of Friar Park. In Idle hands, the estate became a playground for a bizarre cast of costumed characters including fellow Python John Cleese and their frequent collaborator Neil Innes. George was such a supporter of Monty Python that he took out a second mortgage on Friar Park to finance their 1978 film *Life of Brian*.

George Harrison – vocals, guitars, synthesizer, handclaps
Richard Tee – piano
Tom Scott – saxophone, Lyricon
Willie Weeks – bass
Alvin Taylor – drums
Emil Richards – marimba

57. HEY! BABY
Ringo Starr

Written by Margaret Cobb and Bruce Channel
Recorded April–July 1976
Released November 22, 1976
Album: RINGO'S ROTOGRAVURE

During the fadeout of "A Dose of Rock 'n' Roll"—the first song on *Ringo's Rotogravure*—he throws in a snippet of Bruce Channel's classic "Hey! Baby". A complete version was the second song on the album.

Channel's original 1961 hit reached the top of the charts, which none of the musicians involved thought it had any chance of doing. The session band included members of The Straightjackets, a group led by Delbert McClinton. "Hey! Baby" got much of its character from a distinctive bluesy harmonica riff performed by McClinton.

Ringo's connection to the song dates back to early Beatle days. During a 1962 UK tour, Channel was the headliner and the not-yet-famous fab four were on the same bill. Backstage one evening, John Lennon asked McClinton to give him tips on playing harmonica. There is a popular myth that McClinton taught John how to play the instrument, but McClinton has said that's not the case. He recalled that John already knew how to play harmonica (his favorite was one he had stolen from a music store) and didn't really need help. Whatever the case, John's harmonica skills were front and center on the Beatles' first two hits, "Love Me Do" and "Please Please Me".

Ringo Starr – vocals, drums
Lon Van Eaton – guitar
Cooker Lo Presti – bass
John Jarvis – keyboards
Jim Keltner – drums
Randy Brecker, Alan Young – trumpets
Michael Brecker, George Young – tenor saxophones
Lewis Delgatto – baritone saxophone
The Mad Mauries – backing vocals, claps

58. MAYBE I'M AMAZED (LIVE)
Paul McCartney

Written by Paul McCartney
Recorded June 1976
Released February 4, 1977
Album: WINGS OVER AMERICA

Unlike George, who had enough unrecorded tunes in his post-Beatles catalog to release the triple-album *All Things Must Pass*, the bulk of Paul's work was already on record. So most of the songs on his solo debut, *McCartney*, were new creations written at his London home and fleshed out in his 4-track studio. "Maybe I'm Amazed", however, was written during the Beatles' final days.

John, George and Ringo all suffered emotional breakdowns and struggled with addiction in the mid-'70s, but Paul had his dark night of the soul in 1970, drowning his bitterness over the Beatles' breakup in Scotch and considering leaving music altogether. "I was depressed," he told BBC Radio 4, "breaking away from lifelong friends. Not knowing whether I was going to continue in music was depressing." It had not occurred to him to carry on as a solo artist.

"Maybe I'm Amazed", about a lonely man and the only woman who could ever help him, is dedicated to Linda, who encouraged Paul to start writing again and maybe even to start over with a new band. First appearing on the *McCartney* LP, the song was considered an instant classic by critics, but it took seven years to become a single. The 1977 live version was recorded in Kansas City during his triumphant Wings Over America tour.

Amazing in its own right, the man who wrote "Yesterday" has said "Maybe I'm Amazed" is the song he would most like to be remembered for.

Paul McCartney – vocals, piano
Linda McCartney – backing vocals, organ
Denny Laine – backing vocals, bass
Jimmy McCulloch – lead guitar
Joe English – drums

59. TRUE LOVE
George Harrison

Written by Cole Porter
Recorded May–September 1976
Released February 18, 1977
Album: THIRTY THREE & 1/3

Back in their early days of performing in Hamburg, the Beatles would do sets lasting as many as eight hours. To avoid repetition and to keep the audience (and themselves) interested, they played any and every song they knew. One of those songs was Cole Porter's "True Love", sung by Bing Crosby and Grace Kelly in the 1956 film *High Society*. "True Love" was nominated for a Best Song Oscar that year but lost out to Doris Day's "Que Sera Sera" from Hitchcock's *The Man Who Knew Too Much*.

As the Beatles did in Hamburg and also had done while warming up in the studio as recently as 1969, George gave "True Love" an uptempo pop revamp and changed a few chords. George joked that Cole Porter "got them wrong."

Including someone else's song on an album amidst his own compositions was something George hadn't done since his *Dark Horse* days, when he recorded the Everly Brothers' 1957 classic "Bye Bye Love", replacing the original lyrics with his own bitter farewell to his estranged wife Pattie.

George's true love now was Olivia Arias, a savvy businesswoman who worked in the marketing department at A&M Records, later moving to George's label Dark Horse. After many long-distance phone conversations, they finally met face to face at a party in October 1974. They would be married four years later on September 2, 1978.

George Harrison – vocals, guitars
Richard Tee – organ
David Foster – electric piano
Willie Weeks – bass
Alvin Taylor – drums

60. UNCLE ALBERT/ADMIRAL HALSEY
Percy "Thrills" Thrillington

Written by Paul and Linda McCartney
Recorded June 15-17, 1971
Released April 29, 1977
Album: THRILLINGTON

Even before Paul released his 1971 album *Ram*, he had the urge to create a nostalgic orchestral version of it. In May 1971, he called upon Richard Hewson, who had written the arrangements for various Apple Records projects, including the scores for "The Long and Winding Road" and Mary Hopkin's "Those Were the Days."

The resulting album was a cut-for-cut instrumental replica of *Ram* with occasional choir participation. Big band, jazz and vaudeville interpretations lent a quaint, old-timey feel to the proceedings.

Among the musicians participating was guitarist Vic Flick, known for having performed the famous James Bond guitar riff (he also recorded a variation of same at the beginning of the Beatles' *Help!*). Other musicians included Clem Cattini, a drummer heard on dozens of hits including the Tornados' #1 hit, "Telstar".

Not knowing what to do with the album, Paul let it sit idle for six years until he came up with the idea to release it under the pseudonym Percy "Thrills" Thrillington. He fabricated an elaborate campaign for the 1977 release of the album, simply titled *Thrillington*, even going so far as to create fake business cards for his mysterious, reclusive brainchild. The album cover was a painting of a tuxedoed violinist with the head of a ram.

Vic Flick – guitar
Steve Gray – piano
Herbie Flowers – bass
Clem Cattini – drums
Jim Lawless – percussion
Carl Dolmetsch – recorders
Uncredited – flute, harpsichord, strings, trombones, trumpets

61. IT'S WHAT YOU VALUE
George Harrison

Written by George Harrison
Recorded Summer 1976
Released May 31, 1977
Album: THIRTY THREE & 1/3

Something that is important to one person might have no
significance at all to someone else. What may be meaningless to
some could be a big deal to others. That is the message behind
George's next single, "It's What You Value". Recorded at George's
estate studio, the song is an actual account of an episode that took
place during his 1974 Dark Horse tour in America.

George wanted drummer Jim Keltner to join him on his tour,
but Keltner declined. He would have been well-paid for his efforts,
but it wasn't a matter of money. After George's repeated pleading,
Keltner ultimately agreed, saying he didn't want to get paid but was
sick of driving their old VW bus. They made a deal that George
would just get him a new car. Soon, Keltner was driving a Mercedes
450 SL.

When the other band members got wind of it, there was
murmuring of "How come he got a Mercedes when all we got was
money?" The lyrics of "It's What You Value" speak of someone
driving a Mercedes which drives his envious friends wild.

George's own passion for cars often saw him hosting parties at
his estate for drivers of the British Grand Prix. Over the years, his
stable of vehicles included a Jaguar, a Ferrari, an Aston Martin, and
one of the first McLaren F1 supercars ever built, as well as a Light
Car Company Rocket, one of only 55 made.

George Harrison – vocals, guitars, cowbell, tambourine
Richard Tee – piano
Tom Scott – horns
Willie Weeks – bass
Alvin Taylor – drums
Emil Richards – marimba

62. SEASIDE WOMAN
Suzy and the Red Stripes
(Linda McCartney and Wings)

Written by Linda McCartney
Recorded November 27, 1972
Released May 31, 1977
Album: WIDE PRAIRIE

Upon the release of Paul's first solo single, "Another Day" in 1971, his publishing company took legal action against Paul because Linda had been credited as the co-writer. They alleged that Linda was not a songwriter and that the McCartneys were cheating to claim a larger portion of the publishing royalties. To prove otherwise, Paul suggested Linda write a song on her own. The result was the reggae-flavored "Seaside Woman".

In those early years, most of Paul's riches were tied up in post-Beatles red tape. For a while, he and Linda lived off the money she had saved from her work as a rock photographer. They said that if they ever went broke, they would move to the Caribbean and live in a shack. A 1971 vacation in Jamaica gave Linda the inspiration she needed to come up with "Seaside Woman".

Recorded during the *Red Rose Speedway* sessions in 1972, the song was released as a single five years later under the pseudonym Suzy & the Red Stripes. In Jamaica, the locals—inspired by the song "Susie Q" (sic)—gave Linda the nickname "Susie". Red Stripe, meanwhile, is a beer made in Kingston. Paul had planned to do an entire album under the name Suzy & the Red Stripes, but it never materialized.

In 1979, an award-winning music video for "Seaside Woman", animated by Oscar Grillo, was shown in some movie theaters during previews.

Linda McCartney – vocals, electric piano
Paul McCartney – backing vocals, bass
Denny Laine – backing vocals, guitar, piano
Henry McCullough – guitar
Denny Seiwell – drums

63. WINGS
Ringo Starr

Written by Richard Starkey and Vini Poncia
Recorded June 1977
Released August 26, 1977
Album: RINGO THE 4th

No one could be faulted for thinking Ringo's next single might have something to do with Paul McCartney's band, but the song had no connection to his fellow ex-Beatle. A somewhat dark-sounding declaration of devotion, "Wings" was one of six songs on *Ringo the 4th* that Ringo co-wrote with frequent collaborator Vini Poncia.

A veteran songwriter and producer, Poncia first came to Ringo's attention through Phil Spector, for whom Poncia had written songs recorded by the Ronettes and other Spector artists. In addition to working with Ringo on several of his albums, Poncia also produced projects for Melissa Manchester and Kiss.

Ringo the 4th was actually Ringo's sixth solo album but was so named because it was his fourth for the pop market (his first two, *Sentimental Journey* and *Beaucoups of Blues*, were targeted to middle-of-the-road and country audiences). The cover photo, taken by then-girlfriend Nancy Andrews, depicts Ringo dressed as a nobleman, holding a medieval sword in his hands, with a woman inexplicably sitting on his shoulders. Those legs belonged to British actress Rita Wolf.

Wanting to revisit this song years later as a surprise for Vini Poncia, Ringo recorded a vastly different version of "Wings" and considered making it the name of his 2012 album. In the end, he went with the uncomplicated title *Ringo 2012*.

Ringo Starr – vocals and drums
David Spinozza, Jeff Mironov – guitars
Don Grolnick – keyboard
Tony Levin – bass
Randy Brecker, Michael Brecker – horns
Steve Gadd – additional drums

64. SNEAKING SALLY THROUGH THE ALLEY
Ringo Starr

Written by Allen Toussaint
Recorded June 1977
Released September 16, 1977
Album: RINGO THE 4th

Those who liked to bash the Beatles found plenty to pan on *Ringo the 4th*, often ranked near the bottom of fans' favorite solo albums lists. The album suffers from overproduction and a star performer who was said to merely phone in his part. The music tracks were done without Ringo's involvement. Session musicians reported that he would show up long enough to play drums and sing and then would return to his partying.

"I got involved with a lot of different medications," admitted Ringo, "and you can listen to my records go downhill as the amount of medication went up."

One of the more unfortunate pairings of Ringo and remakes was Allen Toussaint's "Sneaking Sally Through the Alley", released as a single in Australia. Like John Lennon's "Ya Ya", the song had originally been performed by Lee Dorsey. In 1974, Robert Palmer revived it via a funky rendition that became the title track for his solo debut. Ringo's 1977 version, maintaining the disco premise of *Ringo the 4th,* was critiqued as particularly "cheesy and unnecessary."

Ringo Starr – vocals and drums
Cornell Dupree, Lon Van Eaton – guitars
David Foster - clavinet
Richard Tee – electric piano
Chuck Rainey – bass
Steve Gadd – drums
Nick Merrero – percussion
Melissa Manchester – backing vocals
Lynn Pitney – backing vocals
Marietta Waters – backing vocals
Rebecca Louis – backing vocals

65. TANGO ALL NIGHT
Ringo Starr

Written by Steve Hague and Tom Seufert
Recorded June 1977
Released September 30, 1977
Album: RINGO THE 4th

"Tango All Night" was written by Steve Hague and Tom Seufert, members of an American West Coast band with the French name La Seine. The song originally appeared on their 1976 debut album *Like the River* and was a top ten single for them in Holland. Fab Four influences were apparent on La Seine's album, which even included a creative interpretation of the Beatles' "I'm Down".

A playful song about a woman who only wants to dance, Ringo's version of "Tango All Night" was released as a single in Argentina, the country where the tango was born. According to Ringo, producer Arif Mardin had happy feet as well. "The way Arif works is different," said Ringo. "He goes in the booth to get a sound and then he's in the studio with you. I tend to close my eyes [when] I've got the cans on so I can hear everything. If I open my eyes and I can see Arif dancing, then I know we're getting a take."

That same summer, Ringo teamed up with actor Donald Pleasence (*Halloween*), who had written a children's story called *Scouse the Mouse*, about a mouse who moves from Liverpool to America. Ringo sang eight of the songs on the album project, all written by Roger Brown, formerly of Stealers Wheel ("Stuck in the Middle with You").

Ringo Starr – vocals and drums
Dave Spinozza – lead guitar
Jeff Mironov – guitar
Don Grolnick – keyboards
Ken Bischel – synthesizers
Tony Levin – bass
Steve Gadd – percussion
Bette Midler, others – backing vocals

66. DROWNING IN THE SEA OF LOVE
Ringo Starr

Written by Kenny Gamble and Leon Huff
Recorded June 1977
Released October 18, 1977
Album: RINGO THE 4th

The first TV theme ever to reach #1 in the Billboard charts was "TSOP (The Sound of Philadelphia)", a 1974 hit by MSFB and the theme song for *Soul Train,* urban music's answer to Dick Clark's *American Bandstand.* Considered also to be the first disco song to reach the top spot, "TSOP" was written by the veteran songwriting team of Kenny Gamble and Leon Huff, who had penned classics for the Supremes, Wilson Pickett, Aretha Franklin, the O'Jays, and many other R&B groups.

Ringo's version of Gamble & Huff's "Drowning in the Sea of Love" was a far cry from Joe Simon's moody 1971 original. Since other artists were now reviving songs by adding a disco flavor, Ringo put on his boogie shoes. In a nod to the popular "Philadelphia Sound," Ringo's remake features a busy dance beat and frantic strings characteristic of the disco era.

Though produced by master hitmaker Arif Mardin (Carly Simon, Barbra Streisand, the Bee Gees, Queen, Hall & Oates, et al.), neither "Drowning in the Sea of Love" nor any of the album's other singles made a dent on the pop charts. Critics who blasted *Ringo the 4th* expressed that Ringo's voice was simply not suited to disco music.

Ringo Starr – vocals and drums
Lon Van Eaton – guitars
Don Grolnick – keyboard
Tony Levin – bass
Steve Gadd – drums
Lynn Pitney – backing vocals
Marietta Waters – backing vocals
Rebecca Louis – backing vocals
Robin Clark – backing vocals

67. MULL OF KINTYRE
Wings

Written by Paul McCartney and Denny Laine
Recorded August 9, 1977
Released November 11, 1977
Album: WINGS GREATEST

An ode to the McCartneys' retreat in Scotland, "Mull of Kintyre" was a very successful attempt at creating a song along the order of "Auld Lang Syne" and other traditional Scottish singalongs. The chorus, written by Paul, is supplemented by verses co-written with Denny Laine.

The initial recording took place on location at Paul's home in Kintyre. For authenticity, his lead vocal and guitar were recorded outside. In the absence of a pop filter to temper wind noise, an assistant's sock was placed over the microphone. A Scottish band of bagpipers and drummers were hired from nearby Campbeltown. To accommodate the key of the bagpipes, the song—mostly in A—had to shift to D for their contribution. Additional voices were added later in London, borrowing singers from the Alan Parsons Project, who were working in the next studio.

Paul was reluctant to release his Scottish waltz as an A-side because it was so unlike anything else on the charts. But, released just in time for Christmas 1977, it became the biggest-selling single of all time in the UK, a record previously held by "She Loves You".

While Paul still owns a farm in Kintyre, the actual mull (the tip of the peninsula) is owned by two sisters. Thanks in part to this song, their nine miles of scenic coastline today is worth 4.5 million dollars.

Paul McCartney – vocals, acoustic guitar, acoustic bass
Linda McCartney – backing vocals, percussion
Denny Laine – backing vocals, acoustic and electric guitar
Joe English – drums
David Paton, Ian Bairnson – backing vocals
Campbeltown Pipe Band – bagpipes and drums

68. GIRLS' SCHOOL
Wings

Written by Paul McCartney and Denny Laine
Recorded February 1977
Released November 11, 1977
Album: LONDON TOWN

With punk rock on the rise in 1977, Paul felt that his sentimental bagpipe ballad "Mull of Kintyre" would clash with the likes of The Clash. He compromised by issuing a double-sided single so that radio stations could take their pick. While European audiences put "Mull of Kintyre" at the top of the charts for nine weeks, Americans unfamiliar with both a "mull" and a "Kintyre" instead showed a preference for its rocking flip side, "Girls' School".

Originally titled "Love School", initial recordings took place at Abbey Road Studios in London, with overdubs added during Wings' stay in Scotland. Guitarist Jimmy McCulloch, who often complained of not getting to rock out, got to do just that with some Led Zeppelin-like licks. Drummer Joe English built anticipation for the choruses by setting each one up with a shift in intensity.

The provocative song's inspiration came during a vacation in Hawaii, when Paul was reading a newspaper. In the back were ads for stag movies, with titles like *School Mistress, Spanish Doll* and *Kid Sister*. Paul wrote some of them down and created his own collection of lustful lasses to populate an imaginary porno flick about a school with no principles.

The colorful cast includes Yuki, who shows "educational" films in a classroom where the windows are covered. A head nurse named Scala runs a massage service from the teacher's hall. Roxanne puts the kids to bed with a little help from pharmaceuticals.

Paul McCartney – vocals, guitar, bass, percussion
Linda McCartney – backing vocals, piano, percussion
Denny Laine – backing vocals, guitar, percussion
Jimmy McCulloch – lead guitar
Joe English – drums, percussion

69. WITH A LITTLE LUCK
Wings

Written by Paul McCartney
Recorded May 1977
Released March 20, 1978
Album: LONDON TOWN

A dreary London winter that lingered into Spring once again revived Paul's wanderlust. Ever willing to combine a vacation with an exotic recording location, Paul hoped to make Wings' next album in their beloved Caribbean, but a lack of proper studios made him fear a repeat of their African misadventure. Engineer Geoff Emerick suggested the Virgin Islands instead. With that, despite its title of *London Town*, Paul's next album was recorded 4,000 miles from England in Saint John.

Denny Laine, who had visited a floating recording studio in Los Angeles, convinced Paul to charter a yacht and convert it into a studio. In May 1977, the lounge of the *Fair Carol* served as a 24-track facility. Two other boats provided lodging for the McCartneys and their staff. Wings spent a month in Watermelon Bay, making music by day and enjoying moonlit swims at night, all to the amusement of curious dolphins. The album came close to being titled *Water Wings*.

Bearing sonic similarities to Steve Winwood, the synth-driven song "With a Little Luck" was unusually long with its runtime of nearly six minutes. To ensure radio airplay, promotional copies included a 3:13 edit. This first single from *London Town* became Paul's ninth #1 solo hit.

Other than the occasional sunburn, Wings found their undistracted working vacation on the open sea especially freeing. Having recorded in London, Nigeria, Nashville, New Orleans, and now on a boat in the Virgin Islands, Linda joked that their next album should be recorded on a train going through Canada.

Paul McCartney – vocals, electric piano, bass, synthesizer
Linda McCartney – backing vocals, keyboards
Denny Laine – backing vocals, keyboards

70. LIPSTICK TRACES
Ringo Starr

Written by Naomi Neville
Recorded November 1977
Released April 18, 1978
Album: BAD BOY

Not to be confused with the Larry Williams song recorded by the Beatles ("Now Junior, behave yourself!"), Ringo's seventh album was named *Bad Boy* after its titular song written by Lillian Armstrong and Avon Long.

Disappointed with the poor showing of his last two albums, Ringo went in a new direction, with his friend Vini Poncia producing. Unlike *Ringo's Rotogravure* and *Ringo the 4ᵗʰ*, there was no disco to be found on *Bad Boy*. It was also the first of Ringo's pop albums that didn't feature any contributions—songwriting or otherwise—from any of his former bandmates.

The first single from the new album was a remake of Benny Spellman's 1962 hit "Lipstick Traces (On a Cigarette)", written by Naomi Neville, aka Allen Toussaint. One of many songs written under the pseudonym of his mother's name, Toussaint wrote "Lipstick Traces" when Benny Spellman requested a song that featured the same low-voiced hook he had performed on Ernie K-Doe's "Mother-in-Law". An almost identical refrain repeats during the fadeout.

Though it was hoped that Ringo's version would do better than Spellman's original, which only reached #80 on the charts, Ringo's rendition failed to get higher than #127.

Ringo Starr – vocals, drums
Morris Lane – piano
Dr. John – synthesizer
Lon Van Eaton, Jimmy Webb – guitar
Dee Murray – bass
Tom Scott – horns
Melissa Manchester, others – backing vocals

71. I'VE HAD ENOUGH
Wings

Written by Paul McCartney
Recorded May and November 1977
Released June 16, 1978
Album: LONDON TOWN

To balance things out after the laidback "With a Little Luck", the most uptempo song on *London Town* was released as Wings' next single. Coming in at a radio-friendly three minutes, "I've Had Enough" was a straightforward rocker based on the classic '50s formula of three primary chords.

When Wings recorded the music aboard their floating recording studio in the Virgin Islands, Paul had only written the chorus, so much of the song was temporarily just a drum rhythm. The verses and vocals were added months later at Abbey Road in London.

An antithesis to the "we can work it out" sentiments of "With a Little Luck", the lyrics of "I've Had Enough" express being fed up with various unnamed sources of aggravation, including a backseat driver who drives him to drink, a "punctual man" who is rushing him to the point of not getting anything done, and a government that taxes his money to fund warfare.

Unmentioned, but undoubtedly another thorn in Paul's side, was yet another mutiny in his band. Guitarist Jimmy McCulloch quit Wings in September 1977 to join Small Faces. Soon after, Joe English left when his wife was in a serious traffic accident. Her miraculous healing led to English's solo career in contemporary Christian music.

Denny Laine attributed the revolving door known as Wings to the pressure of working in the intimidating shadow of Paul McCartney, something he himself had learned to adapt to over time.

Paul McCartney – vocals, bass
Linda McCartney – keyboards
Denny Laine – guitars
Joe English – drums

72. HEART ON MY SLEEVE
Ringo Starr

Written by Benny Gallagher and Graham Lyle
Recorded November 1977
Released July 6, 1978
Album: BAD BOY

On April 26, 1978, to coincide with the release of Ringo's *Bad Boy* LP, NBC aired an hour-long TV special simply titled *Ringo*. The scripted musical teleplay was a *Prince and the Pauper*-like tale starring the oddly random cast of George Harrison, Angie Dickinson, Art Carney, Carrie Fisher, Mike Douglas, John Ritter and Vincent Price, along with Ringo in a dual role playing himself and his down-and-out "twin" named Ognir Rrats.

The soundtrack of the broadcast featured renditions of "I'm the Greatest", "Act Naturally", the opening of "A Dose of Rock 'n' Roll", "It Don't Come Easy", "Oh My My", "You're Sixteen" and "With a Little Help from My Friends", plus a dance sequence to "Yellow Submarine". Songs from Ringo's new release, *Bad Boy*, included his next single, "Heart on My Sleeve".

The TV special didn't do much to help the song's momentum, however, perhaps in part because "Heart on My Sleeve" had already been a hit just two years prior for its writers, Benny Gallagher and Graham Lyle. The Scottish duo were among Apple Records' first artists signed by the Beatles in 1968. Gallagher & Lyle wrote "Sparrow" and other songs for fellow Apple artist Mary Hopkin, and enjoyed subsequent success writing Art Garfunkel's 1975 hit "Breakaway" and their own singles "Heart on My Sleeve" and "I Wanna Stay with You".

Ringo Starr – vocals, drums
Lon Van Eaton – guitar
Jimmy Webb – guitar
Dr. John – keyboards
Dee Murray – bass
Vini Poncia – backing vocals

73. TONIGHT
Ringo Starr

Written by Ian McLagan and John Pidgeon
Recorded November 1977
Released July 21, 1978
Album: BAD BOY

The third and final single from Ringo's *Bad Boy* album was co-written by Ian McLagan, keyboardist for Small Faces ("Itchycoo Park"). They had recorded their own version on their 1977 album *Playmates*. Rather coincidentally, Jimmy McCulloch would join Small Faces for a brief time following his resignation from Wings.

A music video promoting Ringo's rendition of "Tonight" showed him and Nancy Andrews dancing in the French Riviera. Beyond that video, Ringo had no interest in promoting his album, much less going on tour to support it.

Feeling like he'd failed to live up to his status as an ex-Beatle, he became more and more detached from his music and more attached to his alcohol. Even the cover of *Bad Boy*, photographed by Andrews, was a closeup of Ringo's hand holding a drink. He admitted years later that he and his partying pals were not musicians dabbling in drugs, but rather junkies dabbling in music.

Following the dismal sales of *Bad Boy*, his record companies—Epic/Portrait in America and Polydor in the UK—dropped him. For the first time in his solo career, Ringo was without a record label. He wouldn't release another album for three years.

Asked in 1978 by TV personality Connie Collins whether he missed being mobbed by adoring Beatle fans, Ringo replied, "No, I can't run that fast anymore."

Ringo Starr – vocals, drums
Lon Van Eaton – guitar
Jimmy Webb – guitar
Dr. John – keyboards
Dee Murray – bass
Vini Poncia – backing vocals

74. LONDON TOWN
Wings

Written by Paul McCartney and Denny Laine
Recorded February–August 1977
Released August 21, 1978
Album: LONDON TOWN

One of the first songs recorded for *London Town,* the title track was laid down in London before the project moved to the Virgin Islands, with overdubs added in Scotland. Paul began writing the song in Australia during 1975's Wings Over the World tour and co-wrote the rest with Denny Laine in Scotland and Mexico. The finished product is comprised of two songs, "Purple Afternoon" and "London Town".

Between all of the recording sessions that had taken place in London, Scotland and the Virgin Islands, Paul had accumulated enough new material to put out a double album. He chose not to, however, because *Wings Across America* had been a three-album set and he didn't want to test the financial tolerance of the average record buyer.

By the time of the album's release, Jimmy McCulloch and Joe English had flown from Wings, so once again it was down to the McCartneys and Laine, who were the only ones shown on the cover, dressed for chilly London weather on the front and looking ready to set sail for the tropics on the back.

Besides being largely recorded on a boat, *London Town* was also the first solo album on which Paul co-wrote with anyone other than Linda. Paul and Denny collaborated on five of the album's fourteen songs. In September of 1977, Paul and Linda's son James was born. He too would become a future co-writer.

Paul McCartney – vocals, keyboards, bass
Linda McCartney – backing vocals, keyboards
Denny Laine – backing vocals, guitar, keyboard
Jimmy McCulloch – guitar
Joe English – drums

75. BLOW AWAY
George Harrison

Written by George Harrison
Recorded March–October 1978
Released February 14, 1979
Album: GEORGE HARRISON

George hadn't been heard from musically during 1978, but he had assisted his friends Eric Idle and Neil Innes in the TV special *All You Need is Cash*. Aired in March, the mockumentary covered the rise and fall of The Rutles, a fictitious band parodying The Beatles with brilliant wit and a dead-on soundtrack. Mick Jagger, Ron Wood, Michael Palin and many others lent their talents, but no one was happier than George to poke fun at his own outrageous legend.

George had regained his emotional equilibrium in 1978, the year he married Olivia Arias and became a father (their son Dhani would become an accomplished musician in his own right, as well as a spitting image of George).

Ready to get back to the studio, George looked to his past success for inspiration. He listened to his 1970 album *All Things Must Pass* again and again. Its title song, a somber good-bye to things that are only temporary, found its uplifting counterpart in "Blow Away", the first single from George's eighth album, *George Harrison*.

Written on a rainy day at his 19th-century Friar Park estate, the song was inspired by leaky old roofs that were getting George down until he realized that by letting negativity affect him, he was only giving it power. "Blow Away" promotes love and joy as the wind that disperses despair. After a long dry spell, George was writing again.

> George Harrison – vocals, guitars
> Neil Larsen – electric piano
> Steve Winwood – harmonium, synthesizer
> Willie Weeks – bass
> Andy Newmark – drums
> Ray Cooper – conga, cowbell

76. GOODNIGHT TONIGHT
Wings

Written by Paul McCartney
Recorded January 1978–February 1979
Released March 23, 1979
Album: McCARTNEY II

With Donna Summer and songs from the Bee Gees' *Saturday Night Fever* soundtrack dominating the charts in the late '70s, a visit to a disco persuaded Paul to dip his toes into the dance craze with "Goodnight Tonight". Dabbling with a drum machine in January 1978, he built up a basic track that sat idle for many months while he weighed the wisdom of even putting it out.

Following the departures of Jimmy McCulloch and Joe English, Paul decided not to go the blind audition route again to find replacements. This time he went with the recommendations of loyal Wingman Denny Laine. At a bar, Laine had met session drummer Steve Holley (aka Holly), who had just recorded with Elton John. Laine had also been a guest on *The David Essex Show,* where he was very impressed with house band guitarist Laurence Juber. Problem solved.

With Paul's record company clamoring for a new single, Paul pulled out his year-old "Goodnight Tonight" demo. The latest incarnation of Wings brought new life to the track, with Juber adding flamenco guitar. Holley contributed his own foreign flavor via clay hand drums he had recently acquired in Morocco. Lasers, echo and other disco gimmicks were the finishing touches.

John Lennon said he didn't care for "Goodnight Tonight", but was complimentary of Paul's bass line, which drives the danceable hit.

Paul McCartney – vocals, vocoder, guitar, bass, drums, percussion
Linda McCartney – backing vocals, keyboards
Denny Laine – backing vocals, lead guitar
Laurence Juber – backing vocals, lead guitar
Steve Holley – backing vocals, percussion

77. LOVE COMES TO EVERYONE
George Harrison

Written by George Harrison
Recorded March–October 1978
Released April 20, 1979
Album: GEORGE HARRISON

As musicians know, noodling around with a new sound patch on a keyboard or an interesting effect on a guitar pedal can trigger ideas, melodies, and other creative sparks. "Love Comes to Everyone", George said, was inspired by a guitar effect called "Roland".

Partially written in Hawaii, his second single from the *George Harrison* album was another optimistic ode encouraging listeners to look inside their heart to find the love that will get them through the challenges of life.

By now, his fans and critics knew that any Harrison song about universal love had his trademark underpinning of Hare Krishna. But, because George had adapted to their level of leeway, his new soft-sell spirituality had become more acceptable.

Recorded at his home studio known as FPSHOT (Friar Park Studio, Henley-on-Thames), the song includes a guitar intro by Eric Clapton and a synthesizer solo from Steve Winwood.

George had wanted "Love Comes to Everyone" to be the first single released from his self-titled album, but the hook-rich "Blow Away" got the nod, and did very well. This follow-up didn't make much of a splash, but a cover version in Portuguese ("O Amor Vem Pra Cada Um") by Brazilian singer Zizi Possi became a signature song for her.

George Harrison – vocals, guitars
Eric Clapton – guitar intro
Neil Larsen – keyboards
Steve Winwood – Minimoog, backing vocals
Willie Weeks – bass
Andy Newmark – drums
Ray Cooper – percussion

78. OLD SIAM, SIR
Wings

Written by Paul McCartney
Recorded June 29–July 27, 1978
Released June 1, 1979
Album: BACK TO THE EGG

Seeking to make an album with a bit more edge than *London Town*, Paul hired producer Chris Thomas, who was between projects for the Sex Pistols and the Pretenders. Up until now, only Beatles producer George Martin had been tapped for any McCartney solo projects, namely "Live and Let Die".

The album was originally to be called *We're Open Tonight* after one of its songs, but the cut itself was deemed too mellow to be the album's calling card. Linda came up with the final title, *Back to the Egg*. The two sides of the LP were labeled Sunny Side Up and Over Easy.

With a working title of "Super Big Heatwave", "Old Siam, Sir" was developed into a song during a group experiment. Jamming on other than their usual instruments, Linda played drums, Paul played guitar, Denny Laine played bass, and new Wings drummer Steve Holley played piano. The guitar breaks came about from a chord progression of Holley's and a riff by Laine.

Recorded in Scotland and released as an A-side in the UK, the vaguely Oriental-sounding "Old Siam, Sir" contains equally vague lyrics about a woman from Thailand who comes to London in search of a man, only to receive some kind of bad news from back home. The main purpose of the song, however, is to provide a New Wave-tinged backbeat for a robust raw vocal by Paul, which many listeners hadn't heard since the Beatles' "Oh! Darling".

Paul McCartney – vocals, guitar, bass
Linda McCartney – keyboards
Denny Laine – guitar
Laurence Juber – guitar
Steve Holley – drums

79. GETTING CLOSER
Wings

Written by Paul McCartney
Recorded October 10, 1978
Released June 5, 1979
Album: BACK TO THE EGG

While "Old Siam, Sir" was the UK's introduction to Wings' new album, "Getting Closer" was chosen as the first single for the American audience. Written on the piano around the time of *Band on the Run*, the revived tune got full rock guitar treatment for *Back to the Egg*. With an aggressive new band lineup and a producer with New Wave credentials, "Getting Closer" was equipped to take on more of the characteristics of the other chart hits of the late '70s.

Paul had first worked with producer Chris Thomas ten years earlier when Thomas was George Martin's assistant on the Beatles' White Album (technically *The Beatles*). When Martin took a vacation partway through that album's sessions, Thomas served as an uncredited producer on such songs as "Birthday". The then-21-year-old had helped give the White Album some of the very edge that Paul now sought for *Back to the Egg*.

If Paul needed any additional incentive, the McCartneys' oldest daughter Heather was now a teenager and was very much into the punk scene, even wearing her blonde hair short and spiked. Paul's efforts were more than validated when punk and new wave pioneer Elvis Costello said "Getting Closer" was one of his favorite Wings songs.

The initial studio recording had Denny Laine sharing lead vocals with Paul, but the final version, featuring slightly different lyrics, was resung by Paul.

Paul McCartney – vocals, guitar, Mellotron, bass
Linda McCartney – backing vocals, keyboards
Denny Laine – backing vocals, guitar
Laurence Juber – guitar
Steve Holley – drums

80. FASTER
George Harrison

Written by George Harrison
Recorded March–November 1978
Released July 13, 1979
Album: GEORGE HARRISON

As a youth, George's infatuation with British motor racing saw him writing to all his favorite drivers. He took pride in his collection of publicity photographs sent to him in response.

During his busy Beatle years, he continued to follow racing results and enjoyed keeping track of which drivers grew their hair long like the Beatles. By 1977, he had become close friends with world champion Jackie Stewart along with a great many other top drivers. Now collecting cars instead of photographs, his backstage connections with fast company saw him traveling in much the same circles.

George's love for Formula 1 racing was never more evident than on his third single from *George Harrison*. Written expressly to entertain his racing buddies, "Faster" gets its title from Jackie Stewart's 1972 autobiography. While the song makes direct reference to speed, machinery, crowds and worried wives (and includes racing sound effects recorded at the 1978 Grand Prix), George said it can really be about anyone pursuing their dream amid doubts and obstacles. He credited what he learned from race car drivers about alertness, dedication, and determination for giving him perspectives on life he had never learned as a musician.

When "Faster" was released as a single in the UK, proceeds went to a cancer foundation named after driver Gunnar Nilsson. In a 1979 memorial trophy race in Nilsson's honor, George got to drive one of the Formula 1 cars.

George Harrison – vocals, guitars, bass
Neil Larson – piano
Andy Newmark – drums
Ray Cooper – tambourine

81. ARROW THROUGH ME
Wings

Written by Paul McCartney
Recorded June 29–July 27, 1978
Released August 14, 1979
Album: BACK TO THE EGG

"Arrow Through Me" was the last song on the Sunny Side Up side of *Back to the Egg*. The odd album title, explained Paul, simply meant getting back to the beginning, or back to basics.

Recorded one morning at Paul's farmhouse studio in Scotland, "Arrow Through Me" is one of the more pop-friendly songs on the predominantly rocking *Back to the Egg*. Paul and drummer Steve Holley are the only Wings performing, backed by a horn section.

Paul played a Fender Rhodes electric piano, the lower register of which substituted for his usual bass, achieving a full-bodied sound that would later be praised by Paul Simon.

At the suggestion of producer Chris Thomas, Holley overdubbed drumming at half speed to create unique percussion on normal playback. Holley also contributed a Flexatone, the high-pitched "musical saw" type of effect heard at various points.

A Duke Ellington-like horn section was added later at Replica Studios, Paul's London recording setup in the basement of MPL Communications. As the name implies, it was a replica of Abbey Road Studio 2. (The world's most famous recording studio was often in use when Paul wanted to record, so he had an identical control room made in order to finish the album.)

A saxophone solo was also recorded at this later session, but not used in the final mix.

Paul McCartney – vocals, electric piano, synthesizers
Steve Holley – drums, Flexatone
Howie Casey – horns
Tony Dorsey – horns
Steve Howard – horns
Thaddeus Richard – horns

82. ROCKESTRA THEME
Wings

Written by Paul McCartney
Recorded October 3, 1978
Released August 14, 1979
Album: BACK TO THE EGG

Envisioning what an orchestra would sound like if the traditional instruments were replaced by rock instruments, Paul had Wings do a test recording, multitracking three layers of guitars, bass and drums, creating a monstrous rock orchestra sound that passed the test.

Personally acquainted—and in many cases friends—with the Who's Who of other famous musicians of his time, Paul considered what a rush it would be to gather all the great rock legends together in a "Rockestra." Many phone calls later, he did just that. Members of Pink Floyd, the Who, Procol Harum, Small Faces, Led Zeppelin, and other prominent musicians accepted Paul's invitation. Ringo and Eric Clapton couldn't make it. Jeff Beck was uninvited when he insisted on special treatment. Keith Moon died shortly before the session.

Convening at Abbey Road Studios on October 3, 1978, Paul's all-star band recorded two new McCartney compositions, the instrumental "Rockestra Theme" as well as the music for "So Glad to See You Here".

Released as a single in France only, "Rockestra Theme" won the Grammy for Best Rock Instrumental Performance of the year.

> Paul McCartney, John Paul Jones, Ronnie Lane, Bruce Thomas – basses
> Denny Laine, Laurence Juber, David Gilmour, Hank Marvin, Pete Townsend – guitars
> Linda McCartney, Tony Ashton, Gary Brooker – keyboards
> Steve Holley, John Bonham, Kenney Jones – drums
> Ray Cooper, Tony Carr, Morris Pert, Speedy Acquaye – percussion
> Howie Casey, Tony Dorsey, Steve Howard, Thaddeus Richard – horns

83. WONDERFUL CHRISTMASTIME
Paul McCartney

Written by Paul McCartney
Recorded July 1979
Released November 16, 1979
Album: BACK TO THE EGG

In the summer of 1979, Paul had engineer Eddie Klein rig up a 16-track Studer recorder and an assortment of microphones at his home in Scotland so he could dabble with any new idea on the spur of the moment. Plugging mics and instruments directly into the back of the recorder eliminated the need for a giant control board, much less an engineer to man it.

Paul's intention was purely to indulge in experimentation and perhaps create rough demos, at most. Newly wired for sound, he would start fresh each morning, usually with nothing more than a drum track (recorded in the kitchen or bathroom for ambience), and then develop the song of the day by adding other instrumentation. As the music took shape, lyrics came to mind, and he determined that many of the resulting songs were good enough to release as is.

It was on a "boiling hot day in July" when Paul wrote and recorded what has become a perennial Christmas classic. Following in the footsteps of John's "Happy Xmas (War is Over)" from 1971 and George's "Ding Dong, Ding Dong" from 1974, Paul's "Wonderful Christmastime" was released just in time to join the holiday rush of 1979. (Ringo would join in twenty years later with an entire album of Christmas tunes in 1999, titled *I Wanna Be Santa Claus*.)

"Wonderful Christmastime" was the first single performed solely by Paul since 1971. The other members of Wings lip-synced in a party-themed promotional video.

The festive tune was an instant hit. Every holiday season, Paul earns nearly a half million dollars in royalties from this song alone.

Paul McCartney – vocals, keyboards, synthesizers, guitar, bass,
   drums, percussion, sleigh bells

84. COMING UP
Paul McCartney

Written by Paul McCartney
Recorded July 1979
Released April 11, 1980
Album: McCARTNEY II

While Wings' album *Back to the Egg* was riding the charts in 1979, Paul's experimentation with his rented 16-track setup yielded not just the holiday classic "Wonderful Christmastime" but enough new material for a double album. Paul released his preferred cuts as a single LP called *McCartney II,* a follow-up to 1970's *McCartney,* on which he also played all of the instruments.

"Coming Up" was one of the more guitar-driven tracks on a synthesizer-centric collection of songs. Its peppy message about love, peace, understanding, and a "friend you can rely on" featured sped-up vocals and faux brass. Its whimsical matching video showed ten differently costumed Pauls and two Lindas performing as The Plastic Macs. The multiple personas Paul took on included some of the musicians who had recently played with him on "Rockestra".

Wings recorded a live version of "Coming Up" on the final night of their 1979 concert tour. The positive response it received from the Glasgow, Scotland audience—traditionally a tough crowd—convinced Paul to put the song out as a single. The live version, with full band and a horn section, was released as the B-side of Paul's solo original. Disc jockeys in America preferred the live version, which became a #1 hit. In the UK, Paul's solo version reached #2.

John Lennon said he favored the quirky, infectious solo version. When he heard "Coming Up" on the radio, it took him by surprise that it was Paul. John called it "a good piece of work." Up to this time, he would occasionally hear one of Paul's songs and consider making music again. Paul later learned that "Coming Up" was the song that motivated John to get back in the studio after a five-year absence.

Paul McCartney – vocals, keyboards, guitars, bass, drums

85. WATERFALLS
Paul McCartney

Written by Paul McCartney
Recorded July 1979
Released April 11, 1980
Album: McCARTNEY II

Paul had multitracked over a dozen brand new songs in Scotland, making them up as he went along. He got a bit bored with the process, however, and decided to record a song he had already written. "Waterfalls", one that hadn't been used on the previous Wings album, was his favorite at the time.

The gentle ballad began with a simple vocal and electric piano arrangement, with synthesized strings added later in an effect Paul hoped would emulate a Swiss orchestra on a mountaintop. He later regretted not taking it a step further by doing it in a studio with a real orchestra and George Martin at the helm.

"I Need Love", a phrase which repeats frequently in the chorus, would have been the title had Paul not thought it too ordinary. He also had intended to tweak his working lyrics into something more "serious and sensible," but grew to like them as the recording progressed and kept them as is.

With imagery partially inspired by American tour brochures, the cautionary message of "Waterfalls" admonishes a loved one not to go "jumping waterfalls," but to "please keep to the lake." Additional verses cite other metaphorical dangers such as chasing polar bears and running after motor cars.

An entirely different song called "Waterfalls", a 1995 single by the group TLC, contains a similar message about avoiding risky business. Its chorus likewise advises not to "chase waterfalls'" and to "please stick to the rivers and the lakes."

A music video for Paul's song borrowed a polar bear from Chipperfield's Circus in an elaborate shoot that took place inside an aircraft hangar.

Paul McCartney – vocals, electric piano, synthesizer, guitar

86. TEMPORARY SECRETARY
Paul McCartney

Written by Paul McCartney
Recorded July 1979
Released May 16, 1980
Album: McCARTNEY II

Released primarily for the UK audience, the third and final single from *McCartney II* was another song built from scratch. A frenetic rhythmic sequence Paul created on a rented ARP synthesizer sounded to him like a "space typewriter" and became the basis for this fanciful scenario in which someone needs to hire a (conveniently rhyming) "temporary" secretary.

Like "Paperback Writer", the song is an appeal to a business executive, soliciting their assistance. The person making the request isn't too picky, since he's willing to accept a secretary who's a belly dancer, a diplomat, or a neurosurgeon, although he would prefer that she fit on his stereotypical knee.

Paul had made good use of a secretary in the early '70s when he left Apple and needed someone to manage the abundance of paperwork and correspondence to be handled. While "Temporary Secretary" is not about any administrative assistant he had worked with, the song is addressed to "Mr. Marks", the head of the Alfred Marks Bureau, a recruitment agency in Britain. This was a source of amusement for Paul, because a British comedian shared the same name and Paul found it funny to think of a comedian running such an outfit. The Alfred Marks Bureau was pleased with the publicity and asked to use the song in one of their own advertising campaigns, although Paul declined.

In putting together the eccentric "Temporary Secretary", Paul was influenced by idiosyncratic punk rocker Ian Dury ("Hit Me with Your Rhythm Stick"). Paul was such an admirer, legend has it, that he visited Dury when he developed cancer and gifted him with a million pounds to pay for medical expenses.

Paul McCartney – vocals, synthesizers, guitar, bass, drums

87. (JUST LIKE) STARTING OVER
John Lennon

Written by John Lennon
Recorded August 9, 1980
Released October 24, 1980
Album: DOUBLE FANTASY

When John dropped out of the limelight in 1975, he decreed that he would not make music again until his son Sean was old enough to go to school. In 1980, after a summer vacation with Sean, John was back in the studio to record the album *Double Fantasy*, named after a flower he had seen at a botanical garden in Bermuda.

Unlike the dark church bell that opened his *Plastic Ono Band* album ten years earlier, *Double Fantasy* began with a Tibetan wishing chime.

Though the music of the '50s had been a staple of his early career, John realized he had never written a song that sounded like it was from that era. For his comeback single, he wrote new lyrics for three unfinished songs—"My Life", "The Worst is Over" and "Don't Be Crazy"—and repurposed them into the intro, main verses, and middle eight of "(Just Like) Starting Over".

John referred to the song as the "Elvis/Orbison" track, even making his vocal an affectionate—if tongue-in-cheek—blend of Elvis Presley, Roy Orbison, Buddy Holly and Gene Vincent. He told his engineer to make him sound like "Elvis Vincent."

"(Just Like) Starting Over" was John's biggest hit as a solo artist. It had made it up to #6 by December 8 when he was shot and killed, and reached #1 soon after, where it remained for five weeks.

John Lennon – vocals, rhythm guitar
Hugh McCracken, Earl Slick – lead guitar
George Small – keyboards
Tony Levin – bass
Andy Newmark – drums
Michelle Simpson, Cassandra Wooten, Cheryl Manson Jacks, Eric
    Troyer – backing vocals

88. WOMAN
John Lennon

Written by John Lennon
Recorded August 8, 1980
Released January 12, 1981
Album: DOUBLE FANTASY

John's long-awaited return to the music world was cut short the night of December 8, 1980 when lone assassin Mark David Chapman shot him as he was returning home from a recording session with Yoko. The worldwide outrage and outpouring of grief that followed were unprecedented in all of musical history, and over 50,000 fans gathered at Central Park to honor John with Yoko's request for ten minutes of silence on December 14.

Mourners were provided a little source for solace the following month via "Woman", the second single from *Double Fantasy* and one that offered a message of love from John to all womankind. During his five years as a self-proclaimed house husband, he had found a new appreciation for what women do and an understanding of the demands placed on them by society. While most of his love ballads had previously been specifically for Yoko (some mentioning her by name), John made a point to keep the message of "Woman" universal.

John considered "Woman" the most Beatlesque song on *Double Fantasy*, calling it a "grown-up" version of his 1966 song "Girl". To give the song a Righteous Brothers' "You've Lost That Lovin' Feeling" touch, producer Jack Douglas gave the last chorus a modulation, something rarely heard in Beatle songs.

John Lennon – vocals, rhythm guitar
Hugh McCracken, Earl Slick – lead guitar
George Small – piano, electric piano, synthesizer
Tony Levin – bass
Andy Newmark – drums
Michelle Simpson, Cassandra Wooten, Cheryl Manson Jacks, Eric
    Troyer – backing vocals

89. WATCHING THE WHEELS
John Lennon

Written by John Lennon
Recorded August 6, 1980
Released March 13, 1981
Album: DOUBLE FANTASY

John had once told Yoko that he got tired of being a Beatle because he was "writing music for teenagers." In 1980, at the age of 39, John was intent on writing for adults. The third single released from *Double Fantasy* filled the bill with its mature message about taking time to stop and smell the roses.

While most of John's songs on the album were written in the summer of 1980, "Watching the Wheels" started out in 1977 with the title "Emotional Wreck". As the song developed over the next three years, other working titles included "People" and "I'm Crazy". His first demo recording in 1980 boasted a boogie-woogie guitar rhythm.

The finished product, a midtempo piano ballad, was an answer to everyone questioning what John had been doing during his five-year absence. Simply put, from 1962 to 1975 he had been on the celebrity treadmill and "just had to let it go." In a *Rolling Stone* interview, he explained: "Watching the wheels? The whole universe is a wheel, right? Wheels go 'round and 'round. They're my own wheels, mainly. But, you know, watching meself is like watching everybody else. And I watch meself through my child, too."

John Lennon – vocals, piano, keyboards
Hugh McCracken, Earl Slick – lead guitar
George Small – piano, keyboards
Eric Troyer – synthesizer
Matthew Cunningham – hammered dulcimer
Tony Levin – bass
Andy Newmark – drums
Michelle Simpson, Cassandra Wooten, Cheryl Mason Jacks, Eric
    Troyer – backing vocals

90. ALL THOSE YEARS AGO
George Harrison

Written by George Harrison
Recorded November 1980 and early 1981
Released May 11, 1981
Album: SOMEWHERE IN ENGLAND

George had learned of John's passing early the following morning in a phone call from his sister Louise. Musician Al Kooper recalled that George was visibly shaken and "white as a sheet." Regrettably, George and John had been estranged at the time of his death. Phone calls from Paul and Yoko lifted his spirits, but Kooper made sure George's wine glass remained full throughout the day.

"All Those Years Ago", George's musical memorial to John, was originally not about his fallen friend; rather, it was a song he had written for Ringo to sing on his next album. Recorded a month before John's death, Ringo was unhappy with his vocals and gave the song back to George, who later revised the lyrics into a respectful eulogy.

Aspiring to realize the truest tribute possible, George made it a collaboration by all of the remaining Beatles, their first united work in over a decade. Conveniently, Ringo had already played drums on the track. Paul and Linda sang backup vocals along with Wingmate Denny Laine. For additional authenticity, producer George Martin and engineer Geoff Emerick assisted with the recording. Lennonesque strings reminiscent of John's *Imagine* album provided the finishing touch.

George Harrison – vocals, guitars, organ, synthesizer
Al Kooper – electric piano
Herbie Flowers – bass
Ringo Starr – drums
Ray Cooper – tambourine
Paul McCartney – backing vocals
Linda McCartney – backing vocals
Denny Laine – backing vocals

91. TEARDROPS
George Harrison

Written by George Harrison
Recorded November 1980
Released July 15, 1981
Album: SOMEWHERE IN ENGLAND

As coincidence would have it, George's album *Somewhere in England* was originally set to be released on the same 1980 day as John's *Double Fantasy* album. But after sending his masters to Warner Brothers Records—the distributor for George's Dark Horse label—the company responded that the album wasn't "commercial" enough and exercised their right to reject it and have it reworked.

George reluctantly agreed to drop four of the songs and record new ones to replace them, but between the criticism and John's death, he wasn't highly motivated. The release date was pushed back until the summer of 1981.

In writing the new material, George cheekily attempted to give the songs radio-ready hooks that would appease the record company. "Teardrops", which became his next single, was as catchy and trivial as anyone could ask for. With choruses of "Teardrops, doo doo doo doo doo," it was a radical departure from George's soulful songs in which guitars wept. Keyboardist Mike Moran (who would go on to score *Time Bandits* and other Harrison-produced films) infused the synthesizer-driven song with heavy Elton John overtones.

Despite all efforts to give it commercial appeal, "Teardrops" failed to make the charts. Disillusioned, George would fulfill his contractual obligation with one more album and then take a five-year break from music.

George Harrison – vocals, guitars
Mike Moran – keyboards
Herbie Flowers – bass
Dave Mattacks – drums
Ray Cooper – tambourine

92. WRACK MY BRAIN
Ringo Starr

Written by George Harrison
Recorded November 1980
Released October 27, 1981
Album: STOP AND SMELL THE ROSES

Following the lackluster response to his previous two albums, Ringo returned to the more reliable tactic of involving his Beatle buddies, who hadn't been present on *Ringo the 4th* nor *Bad Boy*. George and Paul both wrote and co-produced material for his new album, *Stop and Smell the Roses*. Other songs were written by Harry Nilsson, Ron Wood and Stephen Stills.

Before his death, John Lennon also planned to participate and had already written two new songs to record with Ringo. Both Ringo and John turned 40 in 1980, but although "Life Begins at 40" was timely, the irony was now too painful. As for John's other offering, "Nobody Told Me", Ringo opted not to include that either, so John's own demo was released as a single in 1984.

George's run-in with Warner Brothers over the unmarketability of his then-upcoming album *Somewhere in England* led him to write "Wrack My Brain". The lyrics, which Ringo could also identify with, reflect the frustration of doing one's best but still not satisfying the expectations of others. All the same, the song says, he'll play the game and come up with something they'll enjoy "as much as TV."

Playing piano on this track was Al Kooper, keyboardist with Blood, Sweat & Tears. His friend Herbie Flowers had recommended him for the gig. When George Harrison initially called Kooper to ask him to play, Kooper thought it was Flowers playing a phone prank on him.

Ringo Starr – vocals, drums
George Harrison – backing vocals, guitars
Al Kooper – piano
Herbie Flowers – bass, tuba
Ray Cooper – backing vocals, synthesizer, percussion

93. PRIVATE PROPERTY
Ringo Starr

Written by Paul McCartney
Recorded July 11, 1980
Released January 13, 1982
Album: STOP AND SMELL THE ROSES

While attending the 1980 Cannes Film Festival, Paul was asked by Ringo to contribute to his upcoming album. Paul agreed and booked time at the top studio in Nice, France to record several songs, including "Private Property".

With lyrics warning any potential romantic rival that "she belongs to me" and that no trespassing is allowed, the doggone-girl-is-mine message of "Private Property" foreshadowed Paul's Top Ten duet with Michael Jackson that would come two years later.

Guitarist Laurence Juber was in awe, watching half of The Beatles performing together. He said it was magical to watch Ringo and Paul interact and that they had a sixth sense about each other musically. Backing vocalist Sheila Casey was impressed that the McCartneys always had their young children with them rather than hiring a nanny.

To promote "Private Property" and two other album tracks, Paul wrote a short movie called *The Cooler*, directed by former 10cc members Godley & Creme. Linda McCartney and Barbara Bach act as dominatrix-style guards at a prison camp where Ringo is thrown into captivity. Paul is among the prisoners already incarcerated. The film would become the official British entry for Short Film at the 1982 Cannes Film Festival.

Ringo Starr – vocals, drums
Paul McCartney – bass, piano
Howie Casey – saxophones
Laurence Juber – guitar
Lloyd Green – pedal steel guitar
Linda McCartney, Sheila Casey, Lezlee Livrano Pariser – backing
    vocals

94. EBONY AND IVORY
Paul McCartney and Stevie Wonder

Written by Paul McCartney
Recorded February 27, 1981
Released March 29, 1982
Album: TUG OF WAR

Piano keyboards were made of ebony and ivory until the 1970s. Since then, they've generally been made of painted wood and plastic, to keep the keys from yellowing and also to save the elephants.

Paul had heard British comedian Spike Milligan talking about pianos, saying, "black notes, white notes, and you need to play the two to make harmony, folks!" Paul appreciated the analogy of brotherhood and resurrected the concept years later while composing the #1 hit "Ebony and Ivory" on his electric piano in Scotland.

As written in the key of E, the melody during the word "ebony" uses only black keys while "ivory" uses white. "Harmony," meanwhile, involves both. Paul said all of that was a happy accident and solidified that his muse must have been in support of the song.

In expressing its entreaty for unity, the line "Oh Lord, why don't we" went through several iterations. "Why can't we" sounded too defeatist. "Why won't we" seemed judgmental. But "why don't we" felt like an invitation.

The real challenge for Paul was coming up with a second verse after he had already said everything he wanted to say. Producer George Martin suggested an instrumental break in a different key, which created renewed ground for repeating the first verse.

Knowing the ideal setting for "Ebony and Ivory" was as a duet with a black artist, Paul's first choice was Stevie Wonder, who enthusiastically agreed. Among other things, the blind musician played drums on the track, worrying studio engineers that he might smash the very expensive microphones on the drum kit. He didn't.

Paul McCartney – vocals, piano, synthesizer, bass, vocoder
Stevie Wonder – vocals, electric piano, synthesizer, drums

95. TAKE IT AWAY
Paul McCartney

Written by Paul McCartney
Recorded February 16–March 23, 1981
Released June 21, 1982
Album: TUG OF WAR

When Ringo requested a new song for his latest album, Paul was originally going to give him "Take It Away". After deciding that the song would suit himself better, Paul gave Ringo two others to replace them. Ringo played drums on Paul's recording, doubling up with legendary studio drummer Steve Gadd to achieve the song's unique rhythm.

The term "Take it away," meaning to commence playing or do a solo, inspired Paul to describe three scenarios in which musicians are valued. In one, a lonely driver with a long way to go turns on the radio. In another, a talent scout discovers a band while at their live concert. Lastly, in an after-hours club, faded flowers seem to be the only remaining audience, but Paul encourages the band to play on because "you never know who may be listening to you."

Participating on "Take It Away" was Eric Stewart, formerly of the Mindbenders ("The Game of Love") and 10cc ("The Things We Do for Love"). He influenced the lush multitracked backing vocals not unlike those on 10cc's 1975 hit "I'm Not in Love".

Early in the recording process, producer George Martin played what was to be just a temporary guide track on electric piano. Paul liked the fills he had done, so they ended up in the final mix.

During the week of the single's release, a music video was filmed starring all the players plus actor John Hurt as a music manager.

Paul McCartney – vocals, piano, bass
Linda McCartney – backing vocals
Eric Stewart – backing vocals, guitar
George Martin – electric piano
Ringo Starr – drums
Steve Gadd – drums

96. TUG OF WAR
Paul McCartney

Written by Paul McCartney
Recorded December 16, 1980
Released September 6, 1982
Album: TUG OF WAR

Both the title and basic theme of Paul's album *Tug of War* were in place before much of the writing began. Paul wanted the album to be a representation of life's ups and downs. Earlier in 1980, he spent nine days in a Tokyo jail and had to cancel his Japanese tour after being arrested for having marijuana in his luggage. Then Wings members Steve Holley and Laurence Juber left the band. Worst of all, his longtime friend and partner John Lennon had been killed.

In the plus column, November 1980 saw the release of his concert film *Rockshow*, a celebrative chronical of his 1976 North American tour. From his heart-stirring tribute to John ("Here Today") to the exuberant "Ballroom Dancing", the songs on *Tug of War* run the gamut of emotions, but always with a sense of hope.

The title track begins with a simple arrangement of vocal, guitar and pizzicato strings as Paul wistfully sings of high expectations that have been derailed. When the band and full orchestra kick in, he envisions a time to come when man will climb mountains and dance to the beat of a different drum. In that orchestral section, a military snare is performed by Campbell Maloney, whose Scottish bagpipe band had been instrumental on 1977's "Mull of Kintyre".

On the album version, "Tug of War" opens with sounds recorded at an actual Tug of War Association championship match. As the song fades out, "Take It Away" fades in, omitted from the single release.

Paul McCartney – vocals, guitars, bass, drums, synthesizer
Linda McCartney – backing vocals
Eric Stewart – backing vocals, electric guitar
Denny Laine – electric guitar
Campbell Maloney – military snare

97. THE GIRL IS MINE
Michael Jackson and Paul McCartney

Written by Michael Jackson
Recorded April 14-16, 1982
Released October 18, 1982
Album: THRILLER

Paul's association with Michael Jackson dates back to the '70s, when he wrote "Girlfriend" for the former Jackson 5 wunderkind. Jackson recorded the song on his album *Off the Wall,* and a version by Paul appeared on *London Town.*

In the early '80s, the two recorded a number of songs together including "The Girl is Mine", the first single from Jackson's epic album *Thriller.* Jackson wrote the song after producer Quincy Jones suggested he create a song about two guys fighting over a girl.

Paul questioned whether recording a duet with the superstar would be perceived as a publicity grab. Just as importantly, would egos clash? As he himself was quoted years earlier on John and Yoko's *Two Virgins* album, "When two Saints meet it is a humbling experience." But Jackson said recording with Paul was the most fun he had ever had in the studio. The two enjoyed laughing and throwing things at each other, and even watched cartoons together.

"The Girl is Mine" was the target of not one, but two plagiarism suits brought by would-be songwriters and a former neighbor of Jackson's. He won both cases after personally appearing in court, where it was determined that he didn't need any help to write hit songs.

Paul McCartney – vocals
Michael Jackson – vocals
Greg Phillinganes – electric piano
David Paich – piano
David Foster, Steve Porcaro – synthesizers
Dean Parks, Steve Lukather – guitar
Louis Johnson – bass
Jeff Porcaro – drums

98. LOVE
John Lennon

Written by John Lennon
Recorded September 26–October 23, 1970
Released November 15, 1982
Album: THE JOHN LENNON COLLECTION

"Love" originally appeared on the 1970 album *John Lennon/Plastic Ono Band*. For many, it had been the most relatable and comforting song on John's emotional collection of raw revelations. He had intended to release it as a single at the time, but "Mother" was chosen instead. Meanwhile, radio stations who had found "Mother" too intense preferred "Love" and gave it significant airplay. The song finally got its official single release in 1982 as a tie-in to *The John Lennon Collection*.

Written in the summer of 1970 in Los Angeles, where John was studying Primal Therapy under Dr. Arthur Janov, "Love" was one of the few songs uncolored by his angry unleashing of childhood baggage. Upon returning to England, he recorded a gentle guitar and voice rendition, and asked producer Phil Spector to play the delicate piano accompaniment.

Unlike the lushly-produced, multilayered harmonies on the Beatles' "Because"—which "Love" has often been compared to—the uncluttered guitar and piano arrangement manages to make the sophisticated chord structure seem less complex than it is. Joined by poetic, childlike lyrics ("Love is real, real is love"), the presentation has a romantic innocence that has made the song a wedding favorite for fifty years.

The original album version was in mono with a piano intro that slowly faded in. For the single release, the stereo mix was given full volume to facilitate radio play. The cover of the 1982 UK single release was taken by rock photographer Annie Leibovitz on December 8, 1980, the day John died.

John Lennon – vocals, acoustic guitar
Phil Spector – piano

99. WAKE UP MY LOVE
George Harrison

Written by George Harrison
Recorded May–August 1982
Released November 8, 1982
Album: GONE TROPPO

By 1982, George was marginally interested in making records and more intent on making movies. Three years prior, he had come to Monty Python's rescue when financing for their film *Life of Brian* dried up and he mortgaged his estate to come up with the millions they needed. Eric Idle quipped that it's "the most anybody's ever paid for a cinema ticket in history."

George's investment paid off to the tune of box office gold and he caught the filmmaking bug, starting his own production company, HandMade Films. The company went on to produce a number of acclaimed British movies in the 1980s including *Time Bandits,* alongside less successful ventures such as Madonna's *Shanghai Surprise.*

As for George's 1982 album *Gone Troppo*, the title (meaning to go off the deep end) says it all. The music business had "driven him mad" and he was ready to get out. He refused to do any interviews for the album. Nor, despite his penchant for filmmaking, would he make a music video to promote its single "Wake Up My Love".

The punchy synthesizer and piano-heavy track followed the same Elton John production formula as "Teardrops", while its lyrics expressed a frustrated plea to receive more light from above. Even George's famous spirituality seemed to be in need of a transfusion.

Gone Troppo fulfilled his contractual commitment with Warner Brothers Records. From this point, he would only release an album when he felt like it, which wouldn't be till 1987.

George Harrison – vocals, guitars, bass
Mike Moran – synthesizer, piano
Henry Spinetti – drums
Ray Cooper – percussion

100. I REALLY LOVE YOU
George Harrison

Written by Leroy Swearingen
Recorded May–August 1982
Released February 7, 1983
Album: GONE TROPPO

Motivated more by obligation than inspiration, George recorded his 1982 album *Gone Troppo* with low expectations and minimal fanfare. Even his brother Peter, who worked on his estate as head gardener, was unaware that George had recorded another album.

Lightening the load with some levity was the second and final single from *Gone Troppo*, a playful doo-wop song written in 1961 by Leroy Swearingen. "I Really Love You" had been a Top 40 hit for The Stereos. George performed a faithful, fun rendition with the help of a trio of soul singers borrowed from Ry Cooder's backup group. Anchored by deep-voiced Willie Greene, "I Really Love You" is a unique addition to the Harrison catalog as there is no guitar in sight.

The opening sound of footsteps were courtesy of percussionist Ray Cooper, who was known to wear big hobnail boots. George had him stomp around the back hallway of his mansion in rhythm to set the tempo. Olivia Harrison said that the echoes which reverberated through the hallways of the huge estate normally made it a challenge to move around when recording was in progress, lest a good take be interrupted by footsteps. In this case, Cooper's clomping was an inside joke to open George's tongue-in-cheek cover.

George Harrison – vocals
Ray Cooper – Fender Rhodes, glockenspiel, "feet"
Mike Moran – keyboards
Henry Spinetti – drums
Herbie Flowers – bass
Willie Greene, Jr. – backing vocals
Bobby King – backing vocals
Pico Pena – backing vocals

101. DREAM AWAY
George Harrison

Written by George Harrison
Recorded May–August 1982
Released February 1983
Album: GONE TROPPO

HandMade Films, the production company George formed after his successful financing of *Life of Brian*, saw its second big success with *Time Bandits*, written by Monty Python's Michael Palin and director Terry Gilliam. Starring Sean Connery, Sir Ralph Richardson and a sextet of time-traveling dwarves, the zany fantasy quickly became another cult favorite. With a production budget of $5 million, it earned $35 million during its initial release.

At one point, George's HandMade Films partner Denis O'Brien pushed to have several of George's songs in the soundtrack of *Time Bandits*, but that idea was scrapped by director Gilliam, who didn't want it to be known as a George Harrison musical. Instead, George recorded one new song used over the closing credits, "Dream Away".

Like the film itself, the lyrics of "Dream Away" are filled with irreverence, rattling off contradictions such as "midnight sunshine" and "silent thunder" and featuring choruses in a nonsense language. Gilliam has asserted that the lyrics reflect the tension that was present due to his unwillingness to include more of George's music.

Released as a single in Japan, "Dream Away" was voted one of the 10 Best George Harrison Songs in a 2010 AOL poll.

George Harrison – vocals
Mike Moran – piano, synthesizer
Alan Jones – bass
Dave Mattacks – drums
Ray Cooper – percussion
Billy Preston – backing vocals
Syreeta – backing vocals
Sarah Ricor – backing vocals

102. IN MY CAR
Ringo Starr

Written by Richard Starkey, Joe Walsh, Mo Foster and Kim Goody
Recorded February–July 1982
Released June 16, 1983
Album: OLD WAVE

Ringo and ex-Eagle guitarist Joe Walsh had been friends since the mid-'70s when they were both part of the Los Angeles music scene. Walsh remembers that when they first met, he proudly told Ringo how he struggled but finally learned to play George Harrison's complex solo from the Beatles' "And Your Bird Can Sing", only to be told by Ringo that the guitar wizardry had actually been accomplished via multitracking. This made Walsh even prouder, having conquered a solo that even George hadn't mastered.

Following John Lennon's murder in 1980, Ringo stopped globe-hopping and retreated to his home in Ascot, England, which he had purchased from John in 1973. He asked Walsh to come produce an album at Startling, his home studio. Originally titled *It Beats Sleep*, the finished collection was renamed *Old Wave*, with a cover depicting a younger Ringo taken in a photo booth.

The disappointing sales of his previous albums left Ringo hard pressed to find a record company that would release *Old Wave*. The only label he could attract was a small German label called Bellaphon, whose top artists to date had been Suzi Quatro and Joan Jett & the Blackhearts. Ringo's single "In My Car" didn't chart but the song did a little better when Joe Walsh released his own version in 1987.

Ringo Starr – vocals, drums, percussion
Joe Walsh – lead guitar, backing vocals
Mo Foster – bass
Chris Stainton – keyboards
Gary Brooker – keyboards
Mark Easterling – backing vocals
Patrick Maroshek – backing vocals

103. SAY SAY SAY
Paul McCartney and Michael Jackson

Written by Paul McCartney and Michael Jackson
Recorded May 1981–February 1983
Released October 3, 1983
Album: PIPES OF PEACE

Like many of the songs recorded in 1981 during sessions for *Tug of War*, Paul's collaborations with Michael Jackson were saved for his follow-up album *Pipes of Peace*.

The duo wrote the #1 hit "Say Say Say" at Paul's London office. Back in L.A., Jackson had his session musicians record a funky version with a horn section providing one of its essential hooks. Bassist Nathan Watts assumed Paul would record his own bass and was floored that his performance was deemed by Paul good enough to leave as is. Vocals were added in London months later.

A popular video was made for "Say Say Say" starring "Mac and Jack" as medicine show con artists. Directed by Bob Giraldi, who had done Jackson's "Beat It" video, it featured cameos by Linda McCartney, LaToya Jackson and actor Harry Dean Stanton.

In a fateful conversation, Paul explained to Jackson how real money could be made by getting into song licensing, as he had done. Jackson said he intended to buy the Beatles' catalog of songs when they became available, and Paul laughed it off, thinking it was just a joke. He wasn't laughing when Jackson did buy it out from under him two years later.

Paul McCartney – vocals, guitars, keyboards, percussion
Michael Jackson – vocals, percussion
David Williams – guitar
Bill Wolfer – keyboards
Chris Hammer Smith – harmonica
Nathan Watts – bass
Ricky Lawson – drums
Linda McCartney, Eric Stewart – backing vocals
Jerry Hey, Ernie Watts, Gary E. Grant, Gary Herbig – horns

104. PIPES OF PEACE
Paul McCartney

Written by Paul McCartney
Recorded October 1982
Released December 5, 1983
Album: PIPES OF PEACE

Paul's yuletide offering for the 1983 Christmas season was the title track from *Pipes of Peace*, an appropriate message for the holiday season with its pipers piping and candles lit for love.

Following advice from George Martin, Paul hired whichever musicians would be best for each song on the album rather than use the same ones on each track. For "Pipes of Peace" he employed a pan flutist, a tabla player, an orchestra, and a children's choir.

The children's choir was especially fitting since Paul's initial intention was to write a song for kids about world peace. The tabla, likewise, bears correspondence to Indian poet Rabindranath Tagore, whose quote "In love, all of life's contradictions dissolve and disappear" is paraphrased in the song.

"Pipes of Peace", nominated for the prestigious Ivor Novello Award for Best Song, lost to the Police's "Every Breath You Take". However, its music video, recreating a 1914 ceasefire on a French battlefield, won Best Video at the British Rock & Pop Awards.

Paul understands that putting a message in music isn't something every songwriter wants to do. "I wouldn't blame someone if they didn't want to get into relevant music. There are a lot of people who don't like all that ... I don't think there should be any necessity to have to be relevant. But if you want to be, good luck to you. And thank you."

Paul McCartney – vocals, piano, drums, knee slaps
Adrian Brett – pan flute
James Kippen – tabla
Linda McCartney – backing vocals
Eric Stewart – backing vocals
Pestalozzi Children's Choir – backing vocals

105. SO BAD
Paul McCartney

Written by Paul McCartney
Recorded September 16, 1982
Released December 5, 1983
Album: PIPES OF PEACE

In September 1982, Ringo and his wife Barbara joined the McCartneys in London for Buddy Holly Week, an annual event that was initiated by Paul. While in town, Ringo reunited in the studio with his former bandmate. "So Bad" was one of two songs on *Pipes of Peace* on which Ringo played drums (the other being "Average Person").

The melody for the romantic ballad "So Bad" came to Paul while at the piano during the winter of 1981. As he developed lyrics for it, he had misgivings about the grammatically incorrect line "Girl, I love you so bad," but "Girl, I love you so badly" just didn't fit with the melody.

Playing the song at home for Linda and his children, he enjoyed crooning "Girl, I love you so bad" to his daughters, but felt a little guilty for leaving out his four-year-old son James, so for his sake, Paul sang "Boy, I love you so bad." Whenever he did, Paul said James would "go all shy and it was lovely." So he worked it into the song as "And *she* said, 'Boy, I love you so bad.'"

A particularly melodic bass line supports a simple arrangement with strong harmonies. Paul sings in a high register to convey the vulnerable message of loving someone so much that it can hurt.

"So Bad" was released as a single in some countries as the A-side to "Pipes of Peace". A new version of "So Bad" would be recorded the following year for the soundtrack of Paul's film *Give My Regards to Broad Street*.

Paul McCartney – vocals, electric piano, bass
Linda McCartney – keyboards, backing vocals
Eric Stewart – electric guitar, backing vocals
Ringo Starr – drums

106. NOBODY TOLD ME
John Lennon

Written by John Lennon
Recorded August 7, 1980
Released January 6, 1984
Album: MILK AND HONEY

While John and Yoko were recording *Double Fantasy* in 1980, they already had its follow-up *Milk and Honey* planned and had parts of it recorded. Yoko chose to wait a respectable amount of time before she released those songs, some still in demo form. Meanwhile, she recorded her own solo album, *Season of Glass*. On the cover of her 1981 LP, a half-empty glass sits next to John's blood-stained glasses.

"Nobody Told Me" was originally written by John for Ringo, who had requested songs for his album *Stop and Smell the Roses*. Unused when Ringo couldn't bring himself to sing it, John's version of "Nobody Told Me" became the first single from *Milk and Honey*.

The album's title had already been decided in 1980 by Yoko. Explaining that she and John considered America "the land of milk and honey," she added how the biblical reference relates to a heavenly promise. After his death, Yoko said it was "almost scary—like someone up there told me to call the next album *Milk and Honey*."

"Nobody Told Me", John's lyrical list of oddities observed in these "strange days," includes mention of UFOs flying over New York. On August 23, 1974, John swore he spotted a UFO hovering above the building next to his and May Pang's apartment. Pang remembers John leaning out the window and shouting, "Come back—take me!"

John Lennon – vocals, rhythm guitar
Earl Slick, Hugh McCracken – guitar
George Small – keyboards
Tony Levin – bass
Andy Newmark – drums
Arthur Jenkins – percussion

107. BORROWED TIME
John Lennon

Written by John Lennon
Recorded August 6, 1980
Released March 9, 1984
Album: MILK AND HONEY and ANTHOLOGY

In June 1980, John's last vacation was a trip that could have taken his life even sooner. Having been told by a psychic that he should take a long journey in a southeastern direction, John chartered a 43-foot yacht to sail from Rhode Island to Bermuda, a 700-mile commitment.

Within 48 hours of what was to be a five-day voyage, the Megan Jaye encountered a terrifying storm with gale force winds that rendered the entire crew battered and seasick. John himself had to steer the vessel for a six-hour stint. He soon found his sea legs and at the peak of the storm could be heard shouting out chanties and cursing the sea gods. John called it the most exhilarating experience of his life. Arriving safely, he was newly empowered and spent the next two months in Bermuda, writing over two dozen songs.

At a local club, John heard "Hallelujah Time" by Bob Marley & the Wailers. The reggae song's mention of living on borrowed time resonated with him after his victory at sea, and he penned "Borrowed Time" from the perspective that he used to live without a thought for tomorrow, but now saw a brighter future.

With a pseudo-ska rhythm, "Borrowed Time" was the second song recorded during the *Double Fantasy* sessions. At the 1:28 break, John emulates horns that he had intended to add later.

John Lennon – vocals, electric guitar
Earl Slick – electric guitar
Hugh McCracken – electric guitar
George Small – keyboards
Tony Levin – bass
Andy Newmark – drums
Arthur Jenkins – percussion

108. I'M STEPPIN' OUT
John Lennon

Written by John Lennon
Recorded August 6, 1980
Released March 19, 1984
Album: MILK AND HONEY

During his self-imposed exile at the Dakota, John hadn't seen the inside of a disco in five years. Newfound liberation during his 1980 Bermuda vacation meant at least one night on the town with his personal assistant Fred Seaman. Waking up the next morning, hung over but invigorated, he wrote the chorus of the spirited "I'm Steppin' Out".

His two months in Bermuda without Yoko (who only appeared briefly to drop off their son Sean) saw John reveling in the revelation that he had escaped the routine of responsibility. The lyrics of "I'm Steppin' Out" portray someone who wakes up with the blues but then realizes he has taken care of business and is entitled to go out and have a good time.

The song actually had its origins in the late '70s in the form of a ballad titled "Real Life". The choruses of that work-in-progress were later developed into John's song "Real Love". The verses, meanwhile, were sped up, reworded, and incorporated into "I'm Stepping Out".

John was eager to immortalize his declaration of independence and made "I'm Steppin' Out" the first song he recorded when he returned to the studio. After a half-decade out of the spotlight, John was genuinely having fun.

John Lennon – vocals, rhythm guitar
Earl Slick – electric guitar
Hugh McCracken – electric guitar
Tony Levin – bass
George Small – keyboards
Andy Newmark – drums
Arthur Jenkins – percussion

109. NO MORE LONELY NIGHTS
Paul McCartney

Written by Paul McCartney
Recorded Summer 1984
Released September 24, 1984
Album: GIVE MY REGARDS TO BROAD STREET

Ever since the Beatles films *A Hard Day's Night* and *Help!*, Paul had wanted to try his hand at screenwriting and perhaps even acting in a film. In the years that followed, John, Ringo and George had all played roles on the silver screen. In 1984 it was Paul's turn in his self-written *Give My Regards to Broad Street.*

Starring Paul, Linda, Ringo and George Martin as themselves, the cast included Ringo's new wife Barbara Bach (who he had met while acting in *Caveman*) in a story about missing session tapes.

The soundtrack saw Paul and company (now missing Denny Laine, the last Wing to take flight) recreating many Beatles and Wings songs. Ringo refused to play the old Beatle songs again—resisting comparison to the originals—but did participate in some of the newer material.

"No More Lonely Nights", the only single released from *Give My Regards to Broad Street*, originated in the studio when Paul was experimenting with playing bass licks through an echo machine. A sequence of notes triggered the initial melody. The midtempo ballad was the last song recorded for the soundtrack album.

Pink Floyd guitarist David Gilmour, who had been part of Paul's "Rockestra" session in 1979, returned to play lead guitar. He told Paul to give his session fee to the charity of Paul's choice.

Paul McCartney – vocals, piano
Linda McCartney – backing vocals, keyboards
David Gilmour – guitar
Anne Dudley – synthesizer
Herbie Flowers – bass
Stuart Elliott – drums
Eric Stewart – backing vocals

110. WE ALL STAND TOGETHER
Paul McCartney

Written by Paul McCartney
Recorded October 1980
Released November 12, 1984
Album: PIPES OF PEACE

Rupert Bear, a popular British comic strip character, predates Blondie, Dennis the Menace, and Charlie Brown in America. Paul enjoyed reading Rupert storybooks to his children at bedtime. The same week that the Beatles broke up in 1970, his company MPL acquired the rights to film a Rupert movie, which became an on-and-off project for over a decade. His song "Little Lamb Dragonfly" on 1973's *Red Rose Speedway* was originally written for the movie.

A full-length animated feature proved to be too demanding, so production for a 13-minute cartoon finally began in 1981. The short film played in theaters as the opener for *Give My Regards to Broad Street*. Titled *Rupert and the Frog Song*, it became a children's favorite when released on home video.

Studio recordings for its signature theme "We All Stand Together" (also known as "The Frog Chorus") began in 1980, with two vocal ensembles and orchestral performers that included acclaimed flautist Elena Durán. In the film, Rupert stumbles upon a choir of frogs (briefly joined by cats) singing the song. The deep voices emulating the lowest of the frogs were sung comically for cartoon effect, presenting an amusing challenge for the classically trained singers.

Paul McCartney – vocals
The King's Singers – backing vocals
St. Paul's Cathedral boys choir – backing vocals
Elena Durán, Pete Swinfield – flute
Pete Beachill – euphonium
Robin Williams – violin
John Barclay – trumpet
Gary Kettel – timpani

111. EVERY MAN HAS A WOMAN WHO LOVES HIM
John Lennon

Written by John Lennon and Yoko Ono
Recorded August 1980
Released November 16, 1984
Album: MILK AND HONEY

Studio executive David Geffen came to prominence in the 1970s by signing acts like Jackson Browne, The Eagles and Linda Ronstadt to Asylum Records. But greater musical success followed in the '80s when he launched his own label, Geffen Records, which became home to Elton John, Peter Gabriel, Aerosmith, and many other hitmakers.

When John Lennon ended his five-year moratorium from music, *Double Fantasy* was to be a concept album exploring the relationships between male and female, yin and yang. Subtitled *A Heart Play*, the album was a musical dialogue with Yoko, who wrote and sang half the songs. Upon shopping *Double Fantasy* around to record companies, John found all the top labels interested until they learned it was a package deal with Yoko. Ultimately, David Geffen took the gamble, which he would not regret. *Double Fantasy* became a massive hit for Geffen Records and won an Album of the Year Grammy.

"Every Man Has a Woman Who Loves Him" was sung by Yoko, with backup by John. This remix, giving John the lead vocal, was released as a single in 1984. John had only sung harmony on the original, so his version has a different melody from Yoko's. It was later included as a bonus track on the CD release of *Milk and Honey*.

John Lennon – vocals
Yoko Ono – backing vocals
Earl Slick – guitar
Hugh McCracken – guitar
George Small – keyboards
Tony Levin – bass
Amy Newmark – drums
Arthur Jenkins – percussion

112. SPIES LIKE US
Paul McCartney

Written by Paul McCartney
Recorded September 1985
Released November 18, 1985
Album: PRESS TO PLAY

Director John Landis, riding high from his successes with *National Lampoon's Animal House* and *The Blues Brothers,* needed a title song for his upcoming Dan Aykroyd and Chevy Chase comedy. Feeling that the wacky spy spoof shared a spirit with the Beatles' *Help!,* he requested a theme song from Paul. "Spies Like Us" became Paul's third cinema-related single in a row, and a top ten hit.

Recorded hastily because Landis "needed it yesterday," Paul originally thought to do a James Bond-like theme, but rather than repeat anything he had already done on 1973's "Live and Let Die", he opted for a drum-heavy track with a distinctive vocal echo.

Recorded at Hog Hill Mill—Paul's new private 48-track studio in a restored Sussex lighthouse—veteran studio producer Phil Ramone (Billy Joel, Chicago, Madonna, et al.) pushed him to give the song more and more gusto. Aside from Splitz Enz keyboardist Eddie Rayner, who contributed synthesizer, Paul played all the instruments himself. Paul's cousin Kate Robbins contributed as a background singer.

The music video promoting the song showed Aykroyd and Chase playing instruments. This prevented it from being broadcast on British television, since UK labor laws prohibited non-musicians from posing as players on video.

> Paul McCartney – vocals, electric guitar, keyboards, drums, bass, percussion, tambourine
> Eddie Rayner – synthesizers
> Linda McCartney – backing vocals
> Eric Stewart – backing vocals
> Kate Robbins – backing vocals
> Ruby James – backing vocals

113. I DON'T WANT TO DO IT
George Harrison

Written by Bob Dylan
Recorded November 1984
Released April 22, 1985
Album: LET IT ROLL: SONGS BY GEORGE HARRISON

Written by Bob Dylan in 1968, "I Don't Want to Do It"—with refrains of "I don't want to make you cry"—expresses the conflict of being torn between choices. At the time, Dylan was weighing whether to leave his wife and young family to go on tour. In the end, he stayed home.

George nearly included the song in his "All Things Must Pass" triple album set in 1970, but Dylan's "If Not for You" was chosen instead, along with a Harrison/Dylan collaboration, "I'd Have You Anytime". When Dave Edmunds ("I Hear You Knocking") was put in charge of producing the soundtrack for the teen comedy *Porky's Revenge!*, he talked George into contributing a track. A new version of "I Don't Want to Do It" was recorded and released as a single to promote the movie. George's mid-'80s rendition was a bit more uptempo than the one he had done fourteen years prior.

Originally appearing on the soundtrack album alongside songs by Jeff Beck, Carl Perkins, and Willie Nelson, "I Don't Want to Do It" was eventually remastered by Giles Martin and Dave Edmunds for the 2009 collection *Let It Roll: Songs by George Harrison*.

George teamed up with Edmunds again in 1985 when the latter was musical director for *Blue Suede Shoes: A Rockabilly Session*. The televised concert featured Carl Perkins, Eric Clapton, Rosanne Cash, George and Ringo, with an introduction by Johnny Cash, Roy Orbison, and Jerry Lee Lewis. It marked George's first public performance in over ten years.

George Harrison – vocals, guitar
Chuck Leavell – keyboards
Kenny Aaronson – bass
Michael Shrieve – drums

114. JEALOUS GUY
John Lennon

Written by John Lennon
Recorded May 24, 1971
Released November 18, 1985
Album: IMAGINE

A lecture about a "son of the mother nature" given by the Maharishi during the Beatles' 1968 trip to India inspired Paul to write "Mother Nature's Child" and inspired John to write "Child of Nature". Paul's song made it to the White Album, while John saved his and reworked it into "Jealous Guy". Originally appearing on his 1971 *Imagine* LP, it was released as a single in 1985.

John was indeed a jealous guy, one of the very reasons Yoko became a fixture in the recording studio during the Beatles' last sessions. Paul has said that John admitted this song was also an apology to him for sometimes being envious of the attention he got.

Recorded at John's eight-track home studio, John is joined by members of Badfinger, along with the Moody Blues' Mike Pinder. Pinder was there to play the Mellotron, but the temperamental instrument caused him to be relegated to a tambourine.

John had so much confidence in "Jealous Guy" that before one of the takes, he said into the mic, "Here's a message to all Northern Song shareholders. Here's another half-million." The song is indeed one of John's most successful and has been covered by over 90 other artists.

> John Lennon – vocals, acoustic guitar
> Joey Molland – acoustic guitar
> Tom Evans – acoustic guitar
> Nicky Hopkins – piano
> John Barham – harmonium
> Alan White – vibraphone
> Klaus Voorman – bass
> Mike Pinder – tambourine
> The Flux Fiddlers – strings

115. PRESS
Paul McCartney

Written by Paul McCartney
Recorded March–December 1985
Released July 14, 1986
Album: PRESS TO PLAY

Paul's ambitious film *Give My Regards to Broad Street*, with a production cost of $9 million, yielded barely a fourth of that at the box office. To give his next album every competitive advantage, Paul recruited hitmaking producer Hugh Padgham, who had scored big with Phil Collins, Peter Gabriel and The Police.

Early in the project, Padgham told Paul that he had awoken that morning from a nightmare in which they had made "a really bad, syrupy album" that ruined his career. Paul said they took that as a warning and committed to making *Press to Play* a strong album.

The first single released was "Press", a techno track with electronic drums, sampled vocal gasps and other techno gimmicks. David Bowie guitarist Carlos Alomar, (who also co-wrote the 1975 hit "Fame" with Bowie and John Lennon) played on several *Press to Play* tracks, including this one. He was concerned about whether his punk-funk guitar solo would meet with Paul's approval. Alomar was reassured when Paul gave a hearty thumbs-up to his second take.

Just before the release of "Press", Paul joined David Bowie, Rod Stewart, Phil Collins and other artists in The Prince's Trust Rock Gala, where he performed "I Saw Her Standing There" and "Get Back". The positive response he received to these songs he hadn't played in twenty years convinced him that it was "okay" to perform the old hits. He would add Beatles favorites to his live repertoire from then on.

Paul McCartney – vocals, electric guitar, keyboards, synthesizer
Eric Stewart – electric guitar, backing vocals
Carlos Alomar – electric guitar
Jerry Marotta – drums
Linda McCartney – backing vocals

116. SHANGHAI SURPRISE
George Harrison & Vicky Brown

Written by George Harrison
Recorded May 1986
Released August 29, 1986
Album: CLOUD NINE

George's theme song for *Shanghai Surprise*—HandMade film's 1986 romantic adventure set in 1930s Hong Kong—was an Oriental-flavored stir-fry of all things Chinese. From its opening gong to irrelevant references to woks, rickshaws, coolies, chopsticks and tofu, the song covered most of the Chinese stereotypes. All it needed was a fortune cookie.

Had George consulted Confucius beforehand, he might have passed on the entire movie project. Generally denounced by critics, Madonna and Sean Penn starred in this romp about a feisty nurse embarking on a *Raiders of the Lost Ark*-style search for stolen opium. George himself played a small role as a nightclub singer.

If *Life of Brian* was George's film company's first blockbuster, *Shanghai Surprise* was its first bomb. With a budget of $17 million, the film garnered less than a sixth of that. At the 7th Golden Raspberry Awards, it was nominated for Worst Picture, Worst Director, Worst Screenplay, Worst Actor, and Worst Original Song. Madonna "won" the Raspberry for Worst Actress.

Even Dark Horse Records didn't have much confidence in the title song, as the single had a limited pressing of only 100 copies, and no soundtrack album was released. The lyrics, a recitation of the movie's plot, were sung as a duet by George and British singer Vicki Brown. The backup band includes members of the Knack ("My Sharona").

George Harrison – vocals, guitars
Vicky Brown – vocals
Prescott Niles – bass
Bruce Gary – drums
Uncredited – keyboards

117. PRETTY LITTLE HEAD
Paul McCartney

Written by Paul McCartney and Eric Stewart
Recorded March–December 1985
Released October 27, 1986
Album: PRESS TO PLAY

Unlike most of the material on Paul's latest album, "Pretty Little Head" wasn't written before going into the studio. In an experiment that had worked in the past ("Old Siam, Sir", for example), the musicians switched their typical roles to explore new ground. Paul played drums, while drummer Jerry Marotta played marimba. With Eric Stewart on keyboards, the trio jammed until they arrived at a groove that would make a suitable backing track.

The working title of the song was "Back to Pepperland" (not to be confused with "Return to Pepperland", a 1987 song that was never officially released but became available on bootlegs). The instrumental remained wordless while electronic drums and other hi-tech bells and whistles were added. The tribal-sounding result eventually inspired Paul's otherworldly lyrics about "hillmen" who emerge from volcanos carrying precious gifts and protecting "your pretty little head." Paul's voice is gruff and almost unrecognizable. Guitarist Eric Stewart came up with the equally eccentric "Ursa Major, Ursa Minor" refrain.

Different from the album version, the UK single of "Pretty Little Head" featured a more dance club-style mix and an alternate lead vocal. The music video opens with a clip of "She's Leaving Home" and portrays a runaway (actress Gabrielle Anwar) who travels to the big city, where she runs into trouble. Hurricane winds provided by the breath of a giant Paul McCartney blow the bad guys away.

Paul McCartney – vocals, electric guitar, keyboards, synthesizer, drums
Eric Stewart – electric guitar, backing vocals
Jerry Marotta – vibes
Linda McCartney – backing vocals

118. STRANGLEHOLD
Paul McCartney

Written by Paul McCartney and Eric Stewart
Recorded March–December 1985
Released October 29, 1986
Album: PRESS TO PLAY

The first song Paul had worked on for *Press to Play* was "Stranglehold". He came into the sessions remembering that it had always been George Martin's practice to start an album with a compelling opening track, and this rocker met that criteria.

The simple trio of Paul, Eric Stewart and Jerry Marotta laid down a solid foundation for the song. Even before overdubs, Stewart said the track sounded great: "I went home feeling very, very happy and got a call, which my wife Gloria answered. It was Paul and he said, 'Tell that bloke of yours that it's bloody good and I'm looking forward to tomorrow!'"

Over half the songs on *Press to Play* were co-written by Paul and Eric Stewart, making Stewart Paul's most utilized non-family co-writer since John Lennon. Released as a single only in the U.S., "Stranglehold" was their first collaboration.

Additional guitars and a great deal of other multitracking took place in the weeks to come, prior to a final mix with heavily echoed lead vocals.

The video promo for "Stranglehold" tells a short story in which Paul and his band perform the song at a bar in Amado, Arizona called the Cactus Club. A young Mexican boy wants to get into the bar but is turned away by the bouncer. Linda McCartney arrives by Jeep and lets the boy enter with her. He eventually joins the band onstage, playing the saxophone that was concealed in his suitcase.

Paul McCartney – vocals, acoustic and electric guitars, bass
Eric Stewart – guitars, backing vocals
Jerry Marotta – drums
Gary Barnacle – saxophone
Dick Morrisey – tenor saxophone

119. ONLY LOVE REMAINS
Paul McCartney

Written by Paul McCartney
Recorded October 1–December 6, 1985
Released December 1, 1986
Album: PRESS TO PLAY

Standing out amidst its rock and techno companions, "Only Love Remains", the only love song on *Press to Play,* was the last tune recorded for the album and the fourth single released. Said Paul, "People who've heard the album say, 'That's the McCartney I like.' So I sorta put it on there for them, and for myself, because I'm pretty romantic by nature."

Paul commissioned Tony Visconti, who had scored the orchestral overdubs for *Band on the Run,* to arrange "Only Love Remains" for strings and woodwinds. With the orchestra members assembled, Paul played them his demo and then they recorded the song live, with him on piano. Overdubs were added later, including a saxophone track that only appeared on the single version.

The lush ballad had its visual counterpart in the black & white album cover that adorned *Press to Play.* Taken by veteran glamour photographer George Hurrell, the old-style image of a lovestruck Paul and Linda was taken with the same box camera Hurrell had used when photographing Hollywood starlets in the 1930s.

Paul McCartney – vocals, piano, classical guitar
Eric Stewart – acoustic guitar, backing vocals
Simon Chamberlain – synthesizer bass
Graham Ward – drums
Ray Cooper – marimba, percussion
Dick Morrisey – saxophone
Graham Ward – drums
John Bradbury – solo violin
Linda McCartney – backing vocals
Kate Robbins – backing vocals
Ruby James – backing vocals

120. GOT MY MIND SET ON YOU
George Harrison

Written by Rudy Clark
Recorded 1987
Released October 12, 1987
Album: CLOUD NINE

When the Beatles were recording covers of songs like "Please Mr. Postman" and "Roll Over Beethoven" for their early albums, George wanted to do a version of James Ray's 1963 single "Got My Mind Set on You", but it never happened. In 1987, fresh from a five-year break from music, George was ready to get back in the studio and included the long-awaited remake on his new album, *Cloud Nine*.

The song was written by Rudy Clark, who also wrote "It's in His Kiss (The Shoop Shoop Song)" and co-wrote the Rascals' hit "Good Lovin'". George's lively take on "Got My Mind Set on You" featured a big drum sound and a dozen layered saxophones. He intentionally left out a verse in the original song about misery and bad luck with love. Under the direction of George's new friend and producer Jeff Lynne, the song was a catchy, hook-rich production designed to play well with other radio hits of the late '80s.

Warner Brothers was thrilled with the new improved George Harrison, who not only gave them an album that met their sales potential standards but was willing to help them promote it. George provided them with not one, but two music videos for this song.

"Got My Mind Set on You", the first single from *Cloud Nine*, became George's third #1 solo hit, following 1970's "My Sweet Lord" and 1973's "Give Me Love (Give Me Peace on Earth)". To date, it also remains the last #1 single by any ex-Beatle.

George Harrison – vocals, guitars
Jeff Lynne – keyboards, bass
Jim Keltner – drums
Jim Horn – saxophones
Ray Cooper – percussion

121. CLOUD 9
George Harrison

Written by George Harrison
Recorded 1987
Released November 2, 1987
Album: CLOUD NINE

The title single from George's first album in five years met all the criteria for a strong opening song. Featuring the star-studded lineup of Eric Clapton on guitar, Elton John on keyboards, Jeff Lynne on bass, and session legends Jim Keltner and Jim Horn on drums and saxophone, "Cloud 9" was an invitation to explore George's latest revelations and revisit his recollections with him.

"Have my love," he sings, and "take my time, I'll show you Cloud 9." Even as he extends the optimistic offer, it comes with the acknowledgment that his dream is not all perfection. With that in mind, he suggests taking only what feels right, bailing out as necessary, and leaving the rest for him to deal with.

In his autobiography *I Me Mine – The Extended Edition*, George explained that the song is for everybody looking for something good. "If there's any love around, you can have it," he said, "but if there's any bad about, well, I'll keep that bit from you." The bluesy, moody musical backdrop consisting of only minor chords promotes the dark side of those sentiments.

Released as a single to rock stations, "Cloud 9" was the first song recorded for the new album and was written as early as 1983. Listeners noted that George's voice had deepened with maturity at the age of 44.

George Harrison – vocals, guitars, slide guitar
Jeff Lynne – bass
Elton John – electric piano
Jim Keltner – drums
Eric Clapton – lead guitar
Jim Horn – baritone saxophones
Ray Cooper – percussion

122. THE DEVIL'S RADIO
George Harrison

Written by George Harrison
Recorded 1987
Released November 2, 1987
Album: CLOUD NINE

While driving Dhani to school in the mornings, George would pass a small church. One day, the billboard out front read: "Gossip: The Devil's Radio—don't be a broadcaster." Himself a vocal opponent of mistruth, George resonated with the sentiment and came to write "The Devil's Radio" while en route to a Eurythmics concert. It was released as a promo single to radio stations.

In the early days of the Beatles, George despised it when fan magazines concocted untruths about them. He found the Saturday morning Beatles cartoons particularly nauseating in their fallacy. In later years, buzz about a Beatles reunion needled him endlessly. When he'd rebut those rumors, they would then be replaced with exaggerated reports of feuds between the ex-Beatles, not helping what was already a generally awkward relationship between him and Paul.

Particularly offensive to George had been a stage musical called *John, Paul, George, Ringo & Bert*. In it, a character presents the history of the Beatles in a preposterous account that includes such delusions as a reincarnated Hitler. George was so offended at the London premiere that he walked out at intermission lest he throttle someone on stage. He succeeded in having his song "Here Comes the Sun" removed from the production. Paul likewise expressed his disdain by preventing the show from being made into a film.

George Harrison – vocals, guitar
Jeff Lynne – keyboards, bass, backing vocals
Elton John – piano
Ringo Starr – drums
Eric Clapton – lead guitar
Ray Cooper – percussion

123. ONCE UPON A LONG AGO
Paul McCartney

Written by Paul McCartney
Recorded March 11-12, 1987
Released November 16, 1987
Album: ALL THE BEST (UK)

Paul's 1987 greatest hits collection *All the Best* was released in two versions—one for American buyers and one for the British market, containing what had been the favorites on each side of the pond. In Britain, EMI had high enough hopes for "Once Upon a Long Ago" that it included the brand new track on *All the Best*, gambling that it would become a hit in the UK. It would.

Paul began writing the song in August 1986, reportedly as a duet to sing with Freddie Mercury. The two had become friends following 1985's Live Aid benefit concert. It's hard to imagine Queen's lead singer sharing vocals about puppy dog tails and blowing up balloons, but stranger things have happened ("Bicycle Race", for one). In any case, Mercury had other priorities, so Paul recorded the song himself.

There is an unconfirmed rumor that director Rob Reiner had originally commissioned Paul to write the song for his movie *The Princess Bride*. Released in the UK the same month as Reiner's fairy tale saga, one can imagine how "Once Upon a Long Ago" would invite such speculation.

Paul's sentimental ballad helped propel his UK greatest hits album into the top ten and double platinum status.

Paul McCartney – vocals, piano, guitars, bass, synthesizer
Linda McCartney – backing vocals, tambourine
Nick Glennie-Smith – keyboards
Tim Renwick – acoustic guitar
Nigel Kennedy – electric violin
Stan Sulzmann – saxophone
Adrian Brett – flute
Henry Spinetti – drums

124. WHEN WE WAS FAB
George Harrison

Written by George Harrison and Jeff Lynne
Recorded 1987
Released January 25, 1988
Album: CLOUD NINE

"Aussie Fab" was the working title for this song until George and ELO's Jeff Lynne developed it into a tongue-in-cheek retelling of the Fab Four legend. The lyrics allude to their tax problems, groupies who were left in the dust, and forever being under the microscope of the press. To keep things lighthearted, the new title, "When We Were Fab", was changed to "When We Was Fab" at the suggestion of Beatles press officer Derek Taylor.

Chordal and sonic similarities to Beatles songs including "Glass Onion", "A Day in the Life" and "I Am the Walrus" abound in a production that is convincingly Fab Four circa 1967. George also chooses to mention a Bob Dylan song ("It's All Over Now, Baby Blue") and Smokey Robinson's "You've Really Got a Hold on Me".

When George began writing the song, he had Ringo in mind with a countdown of "One, two" that then erupts into the pounding rhythm that begins "When We Was Fab". This accounts for the fingers seen at the beginning of the music video, doing a one-two leadoff. From there, the video shows George playing the song as a street musician with Ringo, Jeff Lynne and Gary Wright engaged in various activities around him. Passersby include Elton John, Paul Simon, and Beatles road manager Neil Aspinall carrying John Lennon's *Imagine* LP. Paul was unavailable for the video, so they included an unidentified person in a walrus costume playing bass left-handed.

George Harrison – vocals, guitars, keyboards, sitar
Jeff Lynne – keyboards, bass, backing vocals
Gary Wright – piano
Ringo Starr – drums
Bobby Kok – cello

125. THIS IS LOVE
George Harrison

Written by George Harrison and Jeff Lynne
Recorded Early 1987
Released June 13, 1988
Album: CLOUD NINE

George got to know Electric Light Orchestra frontman Jeff Lynne through their mutual friend, singer Dave Edmunds. Lynne had been a Beatles fan from the beginning, and many of ELO's hits were classified as Beatles Fusion.

ELO had recently split up when George told Lynne he was planning to record a new album, and Lynne offered to "help a bit." As someone who knew how to bring out the best in George's sound, Lynne ended up being his co-producer and would play a role in most of George's music from then on.

During his days as a Beatle, George wrote all of his own songs alone, never co-writing with John nor Paul. In 1987, Lynne became George's first real collaborator. "This Is Love", the third single from *Cloud Nine*, was a breezy pop tune with a soft-sell message that love conquers all. One of the song's calling cards is a descending guitar riff foreshadowing Roy Orbison's 1988 hit "You Got It", which Lynne also co-wrote.

Over the course of his lifetime, George would own homes and vacation properties in such far-reaching places as England, Los Angeles, the Swiss Alps, Australia, and Hawaii. For his "This Is Love" promotional video, he filmed at his getaway in Maui. In the video, the denim-clad guitarist sings against a backdrop of breaking waves and tropical vegetation. A joyful picnic nearby features a large assembly of family and friends. The party people include Olivia Harrison, Olivia's father Zeke playing a violin, and Stevie Wonder.

George Harrison – vocals, guitars
Jeff Lynne – keyboards, guitar, bass
Jim Keltner – drums
Ray Cooper – tambourine

126. HANDLE WITH CARE
The Traveling Wilburys

Written by George Harrison, Jeff Lynne, Bob Dylan, Tom Petty
and Roy Orbison
Recorded April 5, 1988
Released October 17, 1988
Album: THE TRAVELING WILBURYS, VOL. 1

Three months into working on *Cloud Nine*, George and Jeff Lynne
mused about creating a band together and how they would want
superstar recording artists to round out the group. Little did they
know that it was about to happen, almost by accident.

For the 12" European disc of "This Is Love", George and Lynne
had to come up with one more song on short notice. In L.A. at the
time, they needed a place to record. Longtime friend Bob Dylan
happened to have a garage studio in Malibu and offered to let them
use it the next day. Roy Orbison, with whom George and Lynne
were having dinner, wanted to come and watch.

George worked out a chord sequence for the song and included
a section for Orbison to sing. Before the session, he had to stop by
Tom Petty's house to retrieve a guitar, and suddenly these five
luminaries found themselves together with a song that needed
recording.

Once united, George got the others to help write his unfinished
lyrics. After being asked for the song's title, he spotted a box in
Dylan's garage marked "Handle with care" and they went with that.

Warner Brothers said the song was too good not to be released
as its own single and requested that the all-star quintet record an
entire album together. The Traveling Wilburys were born.

George Harrison – vocals, guitars, slide guitar
Jeff Lynne – vocals, guitars, bass, drums, cowbell
Bob Dylan – vocals, guitar, harmonica
Tom Petty – vocals, guitar
Roy Orbison – vocals, guitar
Ian Wallace – tom toms

127. END OF THE LINE
The Traveling Wilburys

Written by George Harrison, Jeff Lynne, Bob Dylan, Tom Petty
    and Roy Orbison
Recorded April 1988
Released January 23, 1989
Album: THE TRAVELING WILBURYS, VOL. 1

It didn't take any convincing for George and company to agree to record an entire album together. The only problem was, Bob Dylan was about to head off on tour, so they'd have to act fast. Having written and recorded "Handle with Care" in less than a day, they were confident that they could get nine more songs done with similar efficiency. To that end, they booked ten days at a Los Angeles studio in the home of the Eurythmics' Dave Stewart.

Each day, one of the Wilburys would come in with a song idea which they would all discuss over coffee. Refining it in the afternoon, they would have the song recorded by midnight. Then, according to Tom Petty, they would stay up and be enthralled by Roy Orbison's anecdotes from the golden days of rock and roll.

Following these sessions, George and Jeff Lynne brought the tapes back to George's Friar Park studio where they added more instrumentation.

The last track on the album, "End of the Line", was mostly written by George, although Petty sings the verses. The other Wilburys join in on the choruses, minus Dylan, who was busy preparing to tour. Dylan has been on the road ever since then in what has been affectionately nicknamed The Never Ending Tour. In 2019 he played his 3,000th show.

George Harrison – vocals, acoustic and electric guitars, slide guitar
Tom Petty – vocals, acoustic guitar, bass
Jeff Lynne – vocals, acoustic and electric guitars
Roy Orbison – vocals, guitar
Bob Dylan – backing vocals
Jim Keltner – drums

128. MY BRAVE FACE
Paul McCartney

Written by Paul McCartney and Declan MacManus
Recorded October 1988
Released May 8, 1989
Album: FLOWERS IN THE DIRT

Paul met fellow vegetarian and former Liverpudlian Elvis Costello (aka Declan MacManus) in the early '80s through Geoff Emerick, who was engineering an album for the punk and new wave pioneer. Paul liked Costello's music and the idea of working with a hip, younger co-writer.

Putting their musical heads together at Paul's studio in 1988, they churned out a number of new songs. Four of these collaborations appeared on Costello's 1989 album *Spike*, with six others ending up on Paul's albums *Flowers in the Dirt* (1989) and *Off the Ground* (1993)

Paul couldn't be blamed for experiencing déjà vu during his time with Costello, likening their songwriting approach to his familiar trade-offs with John. Nor could fans be faulted for sensing their own echoes of the '60s in the single "My Brave Face", thanks to an evocative bass hook and Beatlesque harmonies. Paul hadn't played his iconic Hofner violin bass in many years, but Costello urged him to include it on this song. It helped give "My Brave Face" its distinctive character, and Paul has been using it regularly ever since.

Guitarist David Rhodes, best known for his work with Peter Gabriel, contributed electric guitar played with an EBow, which electronically stimulates the strings for continuous sustain. This effect is most evident during the brief instrumental break at 1:49.

Paul McCartney – lead vocals, bass, 12-string guitar, tambourine
Hamish Stuart – background vocals, guitar
Chris Whitten – drums
Robbie McIntosh – guitar
Mitchell Froom – keyboards
David Rhodes – EBow guitar
Chris David, Chris White and David Bishop – saxophones

129. THIS ONE
Paul McCartney

Written by Paul McCartney
Recorded May 18, 1988
Released July 17, 1989
Album: FLOWERS IN THE DIRT

Any song ruminating about regrets has the makings of being a downer, but—ever the optimist—Paul developed the lyrics into an upbeat message about recognizing the promise and potential of each moment. Instead of waiting for a more perfect time that never comes, the right moment is "this one."

Like his father Jim, who enjoyed word-related games, Paul is a longtime fan of wordplay and said "This One" reflects that. "When I heard someone say, 'This one,' I thought it could also be 'this swan.' I liked this image of a swan, like in Hindu art—Krishna and the swan gliding over water lilies. I was attracted to that image, so that's what it became, using the two meanings of the word." The imagery recalls the Beatles' 1968 trip to Rishikesh to study with the Maharishi. For the song's music video, a troupe of female Indian dancers were hired who had to get permission from their mothers to stay out late for filming.

"This One" begins with a surreal opening. To create its otherworldly ambience, Paul had a trio of wine glasses tuned to the notes of G#, B and E for the introductory chord. Having only two hands to spin his fingers around the rims, he borrowed engineer Lance Phillips from the control room to play the third note.

Paul McCartney – vocals, acoustic and electric guitar, keyboards, harmonium, bass, tambourine, sitar, glasses
Linda McCartney – background vocals
Hamish Stuart – background vocals, acoustic and electric guitar
Robbie McIntosh – acoustic and electric guitar
Chris Whitten – drums, percussion
Judd Lander – harmonica
Lance Phillips – glasses

130. OUE EST LE SOLEIL?
Paul McCartney

Written by Paul McCartney
Recorded January 2, 1988
Released July 25, 1989
Album: FLOWERS IN THE DIRT

As someone who himself likes to dance, Paul dabbled with club music from time to time. Following in the footsteps of "Goodnight Tonight" and "Press", Paul tripped the light fantastic in 1989 with "Ou Est Le Soleil?", released as a 12" single to dance clubs.

While vacationing in France with Linda in 1969, Paul overheard someone ask, "Ou est le soleil (Where is the sun)?" Finding the phrase interesting, he and Wings recorded a short demo in 1975 of a call-and-response song not unlike the theme for his 1995 radio show *Oobu Joobu*.

In 1988, working on tracks for *Flowers in the Dirt* with producers Steve Lipson and Trevor Horn, Paul asked if anyone had any ideas. Lipson had programmed a pulsating dance track and played it for Paul, who put a melody to it and revived the phrase from France. The finished product was a hybrid of dance and trance.

Lipson had hoped to receive co-writing credit but agreed that it wasn't a song until it had a melody. Trevor Horn said they didn't spend a lot of time of it because it wasn't a proper song. Paul himself called it "very wacky." The repetitive lyrics answer the title question, suggesting that the sun is "in your head."

More inventive than the song itself is its music video, which replicates a video game with shots of Paul and his band as if they're in Africa, Mexico and under the sea.

Paul McCartney – vocals, drums, bongos, electric guitar, violin
    keyboard, percussion
Hamish Stewart – electric guitar
Chris Whitten – tom toms
Steve Lipson – bass, keyboards, computer programming
Trevor Horn – computerized drums, keyboards

131. CHEER DOWN
George Harrison

Written by George Harrison and Tom Petty
Recorded March 1989
Released August 24, 1989
Album: BEST OF DARK HORSE 1976-1989

George and Tom Petty first met in 1974 at Leon Russell's house and became great friends. Petty looked up to George, likening him to an older brother to whom he could go with any of life's questions and concerns, not to mention someone with vast musical experience and expertise. Their collaborations went far beyond their work together as Traveling Wilburys.

"Cheer Down" was originally intended for George's *Cloud Nine* album. Backing tracks were recorded during those sessions at Friar Park but had no lyrics yet. Many months later, George collaborated with Petty and finished writing them in the course of their Traveling Wilburys activities. "Cheer Down" was one of four songs George gave to Eric Clapton for his 1989 album *Journeyman,* although Clapton only used one of them.

Meanwhile, Clapton was doing guitar work for the buddy cop movie *Lethal Weapon* 2, and convinced George to record his own version of "Cheer Down" for the film. It was used for the closing credits and released as a single.

Co-produced by Jeff Lynne, "Cheer Down" features piano by Lynne's former ELO bandmate Richard Tandy and drums by Deep Purple's Ian Paice.

The song gets its title from Olivia Harrison, who would tell her husband, "Okay, cheer down, big fellow," when his enthusiasm got out of hand.

George Harrison – vocals, guitar, slide guitar
Jeff Lynne – backing vocals, guitar, keyboards, bass
Richard Tandy – piano
Ian Paice – drums
Ray Cooper – percussion

132. POOR LITTLE GIRL
George Harrison

Written by George Harrison
Recorded July 1989
Released October 1989
Album: BEST OF DARK HORSE 1976-1989

George had enjoyed renewed success with his 1987 comeback album *Cloud Nine*. Even so, rather than continue his solo work, he found it more enticing to wait for his Traveling Wilbury bandmates to finish their respective commitments so he could record with them again. In the meantime, he put out a new greatest hits collection, *Best of Dark Horse 1976-1989*.

Unlike the 1976 album *The Best of George Harrison*, which Capitol Records put together at the end of his contract, George personally picked the songs for his new collection, featuring most of his Dark Horse-era hits. Missing were "This Song" and "This Is Love", but in their place were two new compositions.

Released as a promo single, "Poor Little Girl" was the opening track on the new 1989 compilation. It and "Cockamamie Business" were specifically recorded for the album. Jeff Lynne played instruments on both songs, and they carry the trademark Lynne production sound, although only George is officially listed as the producer.

The verses of "Poor Little Girl" tell of a girl with her head in the air and a boy with one thing on his mind, both of whom are looking for love but don't know what love is. The choruses counter with George's admonishment that there is a boundless love he wishes he himself could fully comprehend, much less help others understand.

George Harrison – vocals, guitars, banjo
Jeff Lynne – bass, keyboards, backing vocals
Richard Tandy – piano
Ray Cooper – percussion
Ian Paice – drums
Jim Horn – saxophones

133. FIGURE OF EIGHT
Paul McCartney

Written by Paul McCartney
Recorded December 1987–January 1988
Released November 13, 1989
Album: FLOWERS IN THE DIRT

A Paul McCartney song about romance that expresses the relationship as anything short of bliss is a rarity, but "Figure of Eight" was no silly love song. The lyrics express frustration about the overall unpredictability and unreliability of love, trapping one in a never-ending loop of confusion. Even so, he offers the remedy of taking "good care of each other."

In a 2017 *People* interview, Paul explained, "I liked the philosophy behind the lyrics of this song ... of not being caught in a figure of eight. 'Better to love than to give in to hate,' which now sounds to me like the U.S. elections."

In a two-day recording session at his Hog Hill Mill studio, producer Trevor Horn and computer programmer Steve Lipson challenged Paul to do things he hadn't done in a while, such as singing a rough, loose vocal. In search of a raw and spontaneous vibe, Paul laid down the basic track live with just his voice and bass alongside Chris Whitten's drumming. The rest of the instruments were overdubbed after the essential groove was captured.

The album version of "Figure of Eight" was recorded prior to nailing down the next incarnation of Paul's band. For its release as a single, a new and longer version featured his new guitarists. The song would be the opening number on their upcoming tour.

Paul McCartney – vocals, electric guitar, acoustic guitar, bass,
    celeste, handclaps, tambourine
Linda McCartney – Mini Moog, handclaps
Chris Whitten – drums, handclaps
Trevor Horn – keyboards, handclaps
Steve Lipson – electric guitar, computer programming
Hamish Stuart, Robbie McIntosh – electric guitars (single version)

134. WE GOT MARRIED
Paul McCartney

Written by Paul McCartney
Recorded September 25, 1984
Released February 13, 1990
Album: FLOWERS IN THE DIRT

The oldest song on *Flowers in the Dirt* had been recorded five years earlier, while still in production for 1984's *Give My Regards to Broad Street*. Like "No More Lonely Nights" on that soundtrack, Pink Floyd's David Gilmour provided an electric guitar solo on "We Got Married". Producer David Foster didn't feel that it was a strong song so it was shelved until 1989.

Released as a promo single, "We Got Married" is Paul's tribute to marriage in general and, in particular, his own marriage to Linda. The opening lines, however, were inspired by the teenage courtship of John and Cynthia Lennon. The notion of making love "in the afternoon" was, at the time, a radical concept to the younger and less worldly-wise McCartney.

The minor key song takes a somber look at commitment from the perspective of someone who's been at it for a while. When *Flowers in the Dirt* was released, Paul and Linda had been married for twenty years. The moral of "We Got Married" is "It doesn't work out if you don't work at it."

The album cover, photographed by Linda, is of a background canvas painted by Brian Clarke, who designed the stage backdrops for Paul's 1989-90 world tour.

Paul McCartney – vocals, Mexican guitar, bass, tom, percussion
David Gilmour – electric guitar
David Foster – keyboards
Robbie McIntosh – acoustic guitar
Dave Mattacks – drums
Chris Whitten – percussion
Guy Barker – trumpet
Hamish Stuart – backing vocals

135. PARTY PARTY
Paul McCartney

Written by Paul McCartney, Linda McCartney, Hamish Stuart,
    Robbie McIntosh, Paul Wickens and Chris Whitten
Recorded April 26, 1989
Released November 23, 1989
Album: FLOWERS IN THE DIRT

When recruiting musicians for *Flowers in the Dirt*, Paul was also looking for veterans who could handle the demands of performing on tour. Guitarist Hamish Stuart, formerly with the Average White Band ("Pick Up the Pieces") was recommended and invited to meet with Paul. Unaware of the McCartneys' commitment to animal rights, the stylish Scotsman arrived in London wearing a fur jacket, leather pants and alligator boots. A panicked wardrobe change later, Stuart passed the audition. He had a voice that blended well with Paul's, and it didn't hurt that he sounded a bit like Denny Laine.

Stuart orchestrated the next addition to the band, his guitarist friend Robbie McIntosh, formerly of The Pretenders. Ironically, McIntosh shares the same name as the late drummer and co-founder of the Average White Band, with whom Hamish Stuart had also performed.

Paying it forward, McIntosh in turn suggested keyboard player Paul "Wix" Wickens, who turned out to be the most enduring member of all. Thirty years later, he continues to tour with Paul.

Following long days of recording and rehearsal, the newly assembled band would let off steam by indulging in impromptu jamming. "Party Party" is one of their adlibbed indulgences, recorded live and released as a single targeted to club DJs.

Paul McCartney – vocals
Linda McCartney – keyboards
Hamish Stuart – bass
Robbie McIntosh – electric guitar
Paul "Wix" Wickens – keyboards
Chris Whitten – drums

136. PUT IT THERE
Paul McCartney

Written by Paul McCartney
Recorded April 1988
Released January 29, 1990
Album: FLOWERS IN THE DIRT

According to Paul, his father Jim found standard conversation a bit tedious and was always coming up with unique ways of saying things. When he and his brother Michael asked a "why"-type question for which there was no good answer, Jim would reply, "Because there's no hairs on a seagull's chest."

One of the senior McCartney's most-repeated phrases was "Put it there if it weighs a ton;" in other words, "Take my hand and know that I'm there for you." Paul found it an endearing and comforting sentiment when remembering his father, who died of pneumonia in 1976.

Paul wrote "Put It There" during the winter of 1987 while vacationing at a Swiss chalet. At the end of a day of skiing, he would sit on the balcony with a drink and his guitar. From that peaceful setting came what Paul calls a simple song with a simple message that has a very deep meaning for him. He has been known to get choked up while performing it in concert.

The studio recording benefits from an uncluttered arrangement consisting mainly of guitar, bass and an unidentified string quartet. For percussion, Paul used an old trick he got from Buddy Holly's "Every Day", that of slapping his legs in rhythm. (He said it works best while wearing jeans, because they have the right tone.)

The tuneful tribute to his father was also a nod to Paul's own young son James, born in 1977. Ensuring that his daughters got equal time, the B-side of "Put It There" was "Mama's Little Girl", recorded in 1972 during the *Red Rose Speedway* sessions.

Paul McCartney – vocals, guitar, percussion
Hamish Stuart – bass, percussion
Chris Whitten – drums, percussion

137. NOBODY'S CHILD
The Traveling Wilburys

Written by Cy Coben, Mel Foree and George Harrison
Recorded April 27, 1990
Released June 18, 1990
Album: NOBODY'S CHILD: ROMANIAN ANGEL APPEAL

The Beatles may never have gotten back together, but all four of their wives combined forces in 1990 to lead a crusade to help orphans in Romania. While researching causes she could back, Olivia Harrison discovered that Romanian orphanages overflowed with over 100,000 abandoned children, born when the government forced its women to have multiple offspring to shore up the country's population.

Visiting Bucharest to see where her money would go, Olivia was shocked to find that the orphanages were disease-ridden places where children were neglected. Together with Linda McCartney, Barbara Starkey and Yoko Ono, Olivia created the Romanian Angel Appeal to provide medical, plumbing, and clothing necessities.

Olivia asked George if he would record a single to help raise funds for the charity, as he had once done for Bangladesh. His Wilbury buddies agreed to be on it, and George chose an old Lonnie Donegan song (first recorded by Hank Snow) called "Nobody's Child". The Beatles themselves had recorded a version in the early '60s while backing up Tony Sheridan. George couldn't remember some of the words, so he wrote new lyrics for the second verse.

Ringo, Stevie Wonder, Elton John, the Bee Gees and other musical friends also contributed songs, and the charity album *Nobody's Child* was finished and rush-released within six weeks of Olivia's request.

George Harrison – vocals, guitar
Tom Petty – vocals, guitar
Jeff Lynne – vocals, keyboards, bass
Bob Dylan – vocals, guitar, harmonica
Jim Keltner – drums, percussion

138. BIRTHDAY (LIVE)
Paul McCartney

Written by Paul McCartney and John Lennon
Recorded June 30, 1990
Released October 8, 1990
Album: TRIPPING THE LIVE FANTASTIC

Following the 1980 shooting of John Lennon, none of the remaining Beatles had been in a hurry to get out in front of the public by touring. It wasn't until the summer of 1989 that Ringo kicked things off with his first All-Starr Band, a lineup that featured Joe Walsh, Dr. John, Billy Preston and other notables. Seeing that his ex-bandmate was on the road, Paul felt it was time to get back to where he once belonged.

After his long absence from the concert stage, Paul tested the waters far away from the critics in England and the U.S. by booking the first few months of the tour in Norway, Sweden, Germany, France, Switzerland and Spain. By the time the band hit America and the UK, any kinks had been worked out. Fans lucky enough to get tickets were also gifted with a lush 98-page souvenir book with photos, band bios, concert info, and a plug for Friends of the Earth.

"Birthday", a song that originally appeared on the Beatles' White Album, was written quickly in the studio in 1968. According to John Lennon, it was Paul's brainchild. John roundly dismissed the rambunctious song as a throwaway, but in 1990 Paul knew it would be a crowd favorite enough to make it one of the sixteen Beatle songs on the Paul McCartney World Tour set list. The live version of "Birthday" released as a single was recorded that summer at the Knebworth Festival charity concert in Stevenage, England.

Paul McCartney – vocals, bass
Linda McCartney – keyboard, backing vocals
Hamish Stuart – electric guitar, backing vocals
Robbie McIntosh – electric guitar, backing vocals
Paul "Wix" Wickens – keyboards
Chris Whitten – drums

139. SHE'S MY BABY
The Traveling Wilburys

Written by George Harrison, Tom Petty, Bob Dylan and Jeff Lynne
Recorded April–May 1990
Released November 5, 1990
Album: TRAVELING WILBURYS VOL. 3

The Traveling Wilburys and their serendipitous collaboration were likened more than once to Sun Records' "Million Dollar Quartet" of Carl Perkins, Jerry Lee Lewis, Johnny Cash and Elvis Presley. On a December day in 1956, those four pioneers of rockabilly all happened to visit Memphis' Sun Studios on the same day. A spontaneous jam session was recorded and eventually released.

Years later, Roy Orbison—who had also started out on Sun Records—joined the surviving Quartet members on an album called *Class of '55*. For the elder statesman of The Traveling Wilburys to bring such a pedigree into their ensemble was a solid anchor to the kind of roots music they aspired to revive. George said he got goosebumps hearing the iconic Orbison voice grace his songs.

A month and a half after the release of *Traveling Wilburys Vol. 1,* the album had already gone platinum. Orbison was able to enjoy his return to the charts before he died from a heart attack at age 52 on December 6, 1988. His fellow travelers chose not to replace him, but rather to carry on as a foursome, releasing their second album with the tongue-in-cheek title *Traveling Wilburys Vol 3*. Its bawdy single "She's My Baby" features a solo by heavy metal and blues guitarist Gary Moore.

George Harrison – vocals, guitar
Jeff Lynne – vocals, guitar
Bob Dylan – vocals, guitar
Tom Petty – vocals, guitar
Gary Moore – lead guitar
Jim Horn – saxophone
Jim Keltner – drums, percussion
Ray Cooper – percussion

140. ALL MY TRIALS
Paul McCartney

Traditional, arranged by Paul McCartney
Recorded October 27, 1989
Released November 26, 1990
Album: TRIPPING THE LIVE FANTASIC – HIGHLIGHTS!

Said to originate in either the American South before the Civil War or in the West Indies, "All My Trials" was first recorded as "Bahamian Lullaby" in 1956 by balladeer Bob Gibson. The folk song became a staple of many other singers including Pete Seeger and Peter, Paul and Mary. Elvis famously included it in his American Trilogy medley alongside "Dixie" and "The Battle Hymn of the Republic".

Paul was a fan of Joan Baez' 1960 adaptation of the song, which featured a key change that Paul said he used in writing the Beatles' 1963 song "I'll Get You". In Baez' version of "All My Trials", the line "Hush little baby, don't you cry" goes from D Major to an unexpected A minor, as does "It's not like me to pretend" in "I'll Get You".

During his 1989 world tour, Paul and the band performed this song about the suffering of the poor and struggles coming to an end. The single was released in Britain the same week that Margaret Thatcher was replaced as prime minister, and newspapers implied that Paul's single was a political statement about her divisive economic policies. He said it was pure coincidence, but that he didn't mind shedding light on the plight of the impoverished. On the British talk show *Wogan* he said, "Flinging a little bit of publicity at it I don't think hurts, 'cause the other alternative is to ignore it."

Paul McCartney – vocals, bass
Linda McCartney – keyboard, backing vocals
Hamish Stuart – electric guitar, backing vocals
Robbie McIntosh – electric guitar
Paul "Wix" Wickens – keyboards
Chris Whitten – drums

141. THE LONG AND WINDING ROAD (LIVE)
Paul McCartney

Written by Paul McCartney (credited to Lennon-McCartney)
Recorded April 21, 1990
Released January 4, 1991
Album: TRIPPING THE LIVE FANTASTIC

The long and winding road to get to the Scottish farmhouse Paul had purchased in the mid-1960s gave him the initial inspiration for what became the Beatles' last single and their last #1 song. Originally appearing on 1970's *Let It Be* album, Paul had Ray Charles in mind as he wrote the song in 1968. (Brother Ray did indeed record a version with the Count Basie Orchestra.)

Its melancholy message about longing to find the way back home was especially ironic given the Beatles' breakup. "The Long and Winding Road", in fact, was mentioned by Paul in his 1971 court case as one of the reasons he was dissolving the band. During its recording session, with Paul on piano, John played a half-hearted and errant bass guitar with Yoko by his side. When producer Phil Spector was called in to rescue the recordings, he took it upon himself to add an orchestra and a female choir. Paul felt it was a schmaltzy treatment of his song and demanded that it be reworked, but it was released as is. After enduring months of discord within the band and feeling like he'd lost control, he'd had enough.

Paul came to appreciate the musical arrangement done by Richard Hewson, who would be hired by Paul to orchestrate portions of *Ram*. "The Long and Winding Road" has been a concert staple since 1976. Paul's 1990 single version was recorded live on stage in Rio de Janeiro.

Paul McCartney – vocals, bass
Linda McCartney – keyboard, backing vocals
Hamish Stuart – electric guitar, backing vocals
Robbie McIntosh – electric guitar, backing vocals
Paul "Wix" Wickens – keyboards
Chris Whitten – drums

142. WILBURY TWIST
The Traveling Wilburys

Written by George Harrison, Jeff Lynne, Bob Dylan and Tom Petty
Recorded April–May 1990
Released March 25, 1991
Album: TRAVELING WILBURYS VOL. 3

Olivia Harrison observed that George had a great time recording as a Wilbury because there was no pressure since he and his already-famous bandmates had nothing to prove. The carefree spirit abounds in their final single together, the novelty song "Wilbury Twist". Like Little Eva's "The Loco-Motion", it spells out dance moves in an absurd choreography worthy of the Three Stooges.

At various points, George considered having the Wilburys go on tour in unconventional ways. One idea was to travel by train and do concerts at railway stations. Another would see them flying to exotic locations via an aircraft carrier they would call "The Sponsor Ship" and perform at terminals before flying to the next sunny spot. There had also been much discussion about a third Wilburys album, to be titled *Vol. 5*. Neither the tour nor the album materialized.

Fans at least got to see the non-traveling Wilburys in a promotional video for "Wilbury Twist" starring the band and multiple comedians of the day including John Candy, Eric Idle and Cheech Marin. Filming took place at the palatial Ebell Club of Los Angeles, which has been a popular shooting location for over two dozen feature films (notably *Forrest Gump, The Artist, The Social Network, Wedding Crashers,* and *Ghost).*

George Harrison – vocals, acoustic, electric and slide guitars,
   mandolin, sitar
Jeff Lynne – vocals, acoustic and electric guitars, bass, keyboards
Bob Dylan – vocals, acoustic guitar, harmonica
Tom Petty – vocals, acoustic guitar
Jim Keltner – drums, percussion
Ray Cooper – percussion
Jim Horn – saxophones

143. YOU NEVER KNOW
Ringo Starr

Written by Steve Dorff and John Bettis
Recorded September 14, 1991
Released November 26, 1991
Album: CURLY SUE (soundtrack)

John Hughes wrote and/or directed some of the most iconic young adult films of the '80s and '90s, including the National Lampoon *Vacation* series, *The Breakfast Club*, *Ferris Bueller's Day Off* and *Home Alone*. After completing his final film, 1991's *Curly Sue*, top composer Steve Dorff and lyricist John Bettis were called upon to provide a song for the closing credits.

Playing off the line "You never know which way a day is gonna take you," they wrote a buoyant, nostalgic-sounding song for the Jim Belushi comedy. During the writing, Dorff felt it would be a good song for Harry Nilsson to sing and made that recommendation to Hughes when he played him his piano and voice demo. The director replied that he could imagine Ringo singing it.

Conveniently, Ringo was in Hollywood that week before heading back to Europe, so a session was quickly arranged. In anticipation of Ringo's afternoon arrival, the music track was recorded in the morning. During Ringo's two-hour vocal session, he also chose to overdub a hi-hat on top of the existing drums to give the song more "swing."

Dorff, a lifelong Beatles fan, was in awe hearing Ringo sing one of his songs. In his autobiography, Dorff shares that he told Ringo, "I'm sure you hear this all the time, but you're the reason I got into this business." Ringo smiled and said, "First time today."

Ringo Starr – vocals, hi-hat
Randy Kerber – keyboards
Dean Parks – guitar
Bill Watrous – trombone, whistles
Joe Chemay – bass
John Robinson – drums

144. WEIGHT OF THE WORLD
Ringo Starr

Written by Brian O'Doherty and Fred Velez
Recorded February 1992
Released April 28, 1992
Album: TIME TAKES TIME

In the years that had passed since 1983's *Old Wave*, Ringo recorded no studio albums. Instead, he performed on the occasional George or Paul song, did TV commercials for wine coolers and pizza, became the narrator and played a conductor on the children's series *Thomas the Tank Engine and Friends/Shining Time Station,* started what has become a tradition of All-Starr Band tours, and—most significantly—cleaned up his drinking and drugging. Ringo had seen the effect it was having on his wife Barbara, and in 1988 the two successfully embarked on rehab.

Returning to the studio in 1992, the first single from his album *Time Takes Time* was all about casting off shackles and moving forward. "Weight of the World" wasn't written by Ringo, but its theme of a man and a woman helping each other get through hurdles felt as personal to Ringo as anything he had previously recorded. Musically, the guitar work called up echoes of "I Feel Fine", "Here Comes the Sun" and "It Don't Come Easy".

Ringo put more effort into his new album than he'd had in years. Teaming up in L.A. with producers that included Don Was—whose band Was (Not Was) had the 1987 hit "Walk the Dinosaur"—Ringo's 10th studio album was released just in time to support his second All-Starr tour in 1992. One stop included guest Harry Nilsson in his last public performance.

Ringo Starr – vocals, drums, percussion
Mark Goldenberg – guitar
Benmont Tench – keyboards
James "Hutch" Hutchinson – bass
Roger Manning – backing vocals
Andrew Sturber – backing vocals

145. DON'T GO WHERE THE ROAD DON'T GO
Ringo Starr

Written by Richard Starkey, Johnny Warman and Gary Grainger
Recorded May 1991
Released September 21, 1992
Album: TIME TAKES TIME

Ringo's road to recovery from a lifetime of living large was now starting to be reflected in his own compositions, notably "Don't Go Where the Road Don't Go", co-written with Johnny Warman, who had been a recording artist on Ringo's ill-fated Ring O' Records in 1978.

The song paints a picture of Ringo waking up from a bad dream, unable to remember much about his past. The walls are closing in, his fair weather friends have abandoned him, and he realizes he still has much to learn about looking after number one. He reminds himself that "it don't come easy."

Driving the point home for others to avoid the same dead end, Ringo's drums pound a particularly emphatic beat. Cellist Suzie Katayama, familiar to ELO fans, likewise strikes industrial-strength strokes in this rocker produced by Jeff Lynne.

"Don't Go Where the Road Don't Go" was originally intended to be released as a single in the U.S., but that idea was scrapped. It did make the rounds as such in Germany, however, and Ringo performed it in October 1992 on Arsenio Hall's late night talk show along with the Beatles classic "Act Naturally".

As for the album itself, Ringo said he was more pleased with *Time Takes Time* than any of his albums since 1973's *Ringo*. Reviews were similarly positive, but sales didn't live up to his expectations nor that of his record company, Private Music. Ringo said the music was so private that no one heard it.

Ringo Starr – vocals, drums, percussion
Jeff Lynne – guitars, keyboards, bass, background vocals
Suzie Katayama – cello
Jim Horn – saxophone

146. HOPE OF DELIVERANCE
Paul McCartney

Written by Paul McCartney
Recorded December 1991–July 1992
Released December 28, 1992
Album: OFF THE GROUND

In his attic hideaway one day, Paul was experimenting with a capo high up on the neck of his 12-string Martin guitar. The resulting jangly sound reminded him of Christmas music and cathedral bells. This put him in an elevated frame of mind, thinking about deliverance from darkness, whatever kind of darkness one may be dealing with.

"Homelessness, disease, whatever, big or little, we've all got it," said Paul. "So that was it, really; it just became a kind of optimistic song, either to—perhaps—a girlfriend, or to a God figure. I do like leaving things ambiguous. I've often done that in my songs, so that people say to me, "I always thought it meant something else.""

Only moderately played on American radio, the calypso-flavored "Hope of Deliverance" was a huge hit in Europe, especially in Germany, where it became the most-played song of all time.

A music video featured the band and 350 extras. Much of the shooting took place in Ashdown Forest, the real-life inspiration for Winnie the Pooh's Hundred Acre Wood. In one scene, exploring the forest, Paul is startled by a crow. Despite being in the dark, he wore sunglasses to avoid eye injury when the crow darted skyward.

Paul McCartney – vocals, acoustic and electric guitars, bass
Linda McCartney – autoharp, backing vocals
Robbie McIntosh – acoustic and electric guitars, backing vocals
Hamish Stuart – backing vocals
Paul "Wix" Wickens – piano, electronic drums and percussion, backing vocals
Blair Cunningham – Drums, percussion, backing vocals
Davide Giovannini, David Pattman and Maurizio Ravalico – percussion

147. C'MON PEOPLE
Paul McCartney

Written by Paul McCartney
Recorded December 9, 1991 and June 1992
Released February 22, 1993
Album: OFF THE GROUND

Playing a pleasing guitar riff while vacationing in Jamaica, Paul said "C'mon People" simply emerged from there. He thought of it as very '60s and felt it was "a bit Beatley," which is something he long resisted, thinking he should be doing something different. But, he concluded, to do so could mean dismissing some very good ideas.

An ambitious song encouraging moving on from past mistakes, "C'mon People" was the second single from *Off the Ground*, an album in which Paul wanted every lyric to count. To that end, he had poet friend Adrian Mitchell critique every word. At Mitchell's suggestion, Paul changed "We've got a future and it's coming in" to the stronger "rushing in" and "charging in."

Recording on a Friday afternoon, equipment problems and a sick engineer almost caused the band to wait till Monday to record the song, but they gave it a shot anyway and nailed it in one take.

Wanting a big sound for "C'mon People", Paul asked George Martin to overdub an orchestral score. Even though Martin, now in his mid-60s, was winding down and preparing to retire, he agreed. During that follow-up session at Abbey Road, Paul said Martin conducted with the same enthusiasm and vigor with which he produced all of the Beatle sessions thirty years earlier. Keyboardist Wix noticed that when Martin notated the session date on the song's orchestral score, he unintentionally wrote 1962 instead of 1992.

Paul McCartney – vocals, piano, celeste, electric guitar, whistle
Linda McCartney – Moog, backing vocals
Hamish Stuart – bass, backing vocals
Paul "Wix" Wickens – congas, synthesizer
Blair Cunningham – drums, congas

148. OFF THE GROUND
Paul McCartney

Written by Paul McCartney
Recorded December 1991–July 1992
Released April 19, 1993
Album: OFF THE GROUND

Coming up on age 50, Paul wanted his new album to convey messages that were important to him. Animal rights, vegetarianism and green politics all filter into the songs on *Off the Ground*, with world peace the overriding theme.

Like most of the songs on the album, Paul had created demos from which the band learned the material. In search of freshness and spontaneity, they recorded each track live whenever possible with a minimum of retakes and overdubs. The exception was the title track, which almost didn't make it on *Off the Ground* at all.

It was near the end of the album sessions when keyboard wiz Wix, an electronics buff, suggested experimenting with computer music. Paul gave the rest of the band the day off while he and Wix played with the latest studio toys. One of the songs Paul had written was one he considered to be a folk song that didn't feel right for the album. But if they were going to mess around and possibly waste a song, he figured it might as well be that one.

After a catchy computerized rhythm track was created, Paul got interested. Adding guitars and a synthesized bass, the song came together to Paul's satisfaction with only minor things yet to be added. When he got home that night, he spoke to one of his daughters on the phone, who asked him what he'd done that day. When he told her "Off the Ground", she said, "That's a great album title!"

Paul McCartney – vocals, drums, percussion
Linda McCartney – backing vocals
Paul "Wix" Wickens – piano, keyboards, synthesized bass
Robbie McIntosh – electric guitar, percussion
Hamish Stuart – percussion, backing vocals

149. BIKER LIKE AN ICON
Paul McCartney

Written by Paul McCartney
Recorded November 25, 1991
Released November 8, 1993
Album: OFF THE GROUND

A conversation with Linda about cameras led to the phrase "I like a Nikon." Always primed for a play on words, Paul adapted it into "like an icon" for this upbeat song about a girl who idolizes her motorcycle hero as if he were a religious figure.

"I like confusing titles," said Paul. "John and [I] would always look at the new titles in the American charts and get intrigued by things like 'Quarter to Three' by U.S. Bonds—what could that be about? It was very important to us to get a title that had that buzz. Think of our titles … 'Hard Day's Night', 'Strawberry Fields Forever', 'Penny Lane', 'Fixing a Hole'."

As he had done with "Hope of Deliverance", Paul developed "Biker Like an Icon" in his attic on his 12-string Martin guitar. It was the first song Paul chose to record for *Off the Ground*. Unlike previous McCartney projects, sessions for the album followed a more predictable schedule of Monday through Friday from 12 to 8 p.m.

Avoiding the pattern of spending weeks doing overdubs, the band attempted arrangements that could be easily replicated on tour. After only fifteen minutes of learning "Biker Like an Icon", it was captured live—including vocals—in one take. They listened to it a few weeks later to assess whether it could be improved upon, but as bassist Hamish Stuart reported, no need. The magic was there.

Paul McCartney – vocals, acoustic guitar, percussion
Linda McCartney – keyboards
Paul "Wix" Wickens – piano, keyboards
Robbie McIntosh – slide guitar
Hamish Stuart – bass, backing vocals
Blair Cunningham – drums

150. TRANSPIRITUAL STOMP
The Fireman (Paul McCartney and Youth)

Written by Paul McCartney
Recorded October 7-10, 1992
Released November 15, 1993
Album: STRAWBERRIES OCEANS SHIPS FOREST

English record producer Martin Glover had made a name for himself as bass player for the band Killing Joke before becoming a prominent remix artist specializing in techno and psychedelic trance music. Professionally known as Youth, Glover was invited to Paul's studio during mixing sessions for *Off the Ground*. The two hit it off and began collaborating on a new project of dance remixes from the album.

Using musical loops snipped from selected songs as building blocks and then overdubbing additional instrumentation, entirely new compositions were fabricated. The process was reminiscent of the Beatles' experimentation with tape loops on "Tomorrow Never Knows" and "Revolution 9", except that the latest digital technology afforded much greater creative control.

The resulting nine songs were variations on a single theme, sharing a techno dance beat and elements from *Off the Ground* and *Back to the Egg*. Youth intended to edit them down into one 12-inch dance mix, but Paul loved all of it enough to want to release it as an album. However, the electronica was so far removed from any of his previous releases that he didn't want to shock and possibly annoy fans by putting it out as a Paul McCartney album. For that reason, he and Youth adopted the pseudonym The Fireman.

Despite efforts to keep their identities under wraps, word got out, and most of the buyers of The Fireman's album—titled *Strawberries Oceans Ships Forest*—were McCartney fans. The single, "Transpiritual Stomp", got its title because it made Youth think of a pagan dance with tribesmen kicking up their feet.

Paul McCartney – voice, banjo, flute, double bass, others
Youth – bass

151. FREE AS A BIRD
The Beatles

Written by John Lennon, Paul McCartney and George Harrison
Recorded 1977 and February-March 1994
Released December 4, 1995
Album: ANTHOLOGY 1

A documentary film about the Beatles from their own perspective began in the late '60s as *The Long and Winding Road*, but stalled upon their breakup. The project resurfaced in 1995 as the 13-hour *Beatles Anthology* miniseries and three double albums of unreleased takes.

Paul, George and Ringo all participated and even planned to record new music for the project. But, they contended, they were not the Beatles without John. When it was discovered that Yoko possessed some unreleased demos that John had recorded at home, they wanted to incorporate them, and Yoko consented to provide the recordings.

Of the four songs, "Free as a Bird" was deemed the most promising. Trouble was, the cassette audio was noisy. At George's suggestion, they enlisted Jeff Lynne to clean up the track and turn it into something they could add their voices and instruments to. Paul and George also wrote lyrics for an unfinished bridge.

Being in the studio together for the first time in 25 years was emotional enough, but singing and playing along with John again was almost painful. To temper the trauma, they adopted the mindset that John was on holiday and had left them his song to finish.

"Free as a Bird" went on to win the 1997 Grammy for Best Pop Performance by a Duo or Group. Yoko, who had long been blamed for breaking up the Beatles, said she was pleased to have played a role in bringing them back together.

John Lennon – vocals, piano
Paul McCartney – vocals, acoustic guitar, piano, bass, synthesizer
George Harrison – vocals, slide guitar, acoustic guitar, ukulele
Ringo Starr – drums, backing vocals
Jeff Lynne – electric guitar, backing vocals

152. REAL LOVE
The Beatles

Written by John Lennon
Recorded 1979 and February 1995
Released March 4, 1996
Album: ANTHOLOGY 2

In the late '70s, John started writing a stage musical called *The Ballad of John and Yoko*. Among the songs he intended to include was "Real Love". A year after recording "Free as a Bird", the remaining Beatles reconvened to complete it, making it the second single for the *Anthology* series.

Once again, Jeff Lynne was enlisted to produce in the absence of George Martin, now suffering from hearing loss after a lifetime of extreme audio. Intent on giving the song a true Beatles treatment, Ringo played his legendary Ludwig drum kit, George played his vintage Stratocaster, and Paul played the harpsichord John had used on "Because". To further sanctify the session, he also played Bill Black's double bass—the same one used on Elvis' "Heartbreak Hotel"—which Linda had bought for Paul in Nashville.

Another song from John's demo tapes, "Now and Then", was intended as a single, and an afternoon was spent making a backing track. But the excessive noise level on the cassette, the song's unfinished state, and the fact that George simply didn't care for it, made it too great a challenge, and the idea was scrapped. As recently as 2012, Paul said he plans to finish "Now and Then" someday.

The fourth song on John's cassettes, "Grow Old with Me", would be recorded by Ringo in 2019.

John Lennon – vocals, piano
Paul McCartney – acoustic guitar, piano, harmonium, harpsichord, bass, double bass, percussion, backing vocals
George Harrison – electric and acoustic guitar, percussion, backing vocals
Ringo Starr – drums, percussion, backing vocals
Jeff Lynne – guitar, backing vocals

153. THE WORLD TONIGHT
Paul McCartney

Written by Paul McCartney
Recorded November 13-17, 1995
Released April 17, 1997
Album: FLAMING PIE

Over the course of 1995 and 1996, while the three double album sets of the Beatles' *Anthology* were being released, EMI requested that Paul not put out any solo albums. During that time, he co-founded the Liverpool Institute for the Performing Arts at the now-closed school he and George Harrison had attended as teenagers. He also worked on *Standing Stone*, his second major classical work following the success of his orchestral *Liverpool Oratorio* in 1991.

Paul's band members had gone their separate ways after his 1993 New World Tour, so his next album, *Flaming Pie*, featured a variety of other musical contributors. They included his son James, Steve Miller, Ringo, and Jeff Lynne.

Paul had originally been wary of Lynne's participation in "Free as a Bird" and "Real Love", as his production style was known for adding ELO overtones to everything he touched. But there was no denying that Lynne—heavily influenced by the Beatles—was a kindred spirit who knew how to take the material to the next level. Paul had Lynne produce most of the songs on *Flaming Pie*.

"The World Tonight" was originally a folksy composition, written on an acoustic guitar while Paul was vacationing in America. It speaks of the pitfalls of superstardom, in which paparazzi lurk and everyone wants something from you. He said he didn't know where the line "I go back so far/I'm in front of me" came from, but added that if he had been writing with John Lennon, John would have said, "Leave that one in; we don't know what it means but we do know what it means."

Paul McCartney – vocals, acoustic and electric guitar, bass, piano,
    drums, percussion
Jeff Lynne – electric and acoustic guitar, keyboards, backing vocals

154. YOUNG BOY
Paul McCartney

Written by Paul McCartney
Recorded February 22, 1995
Released April 28, 1997
Album: FLAMING PIE

Working on the massive *Anthology* series, Paul listened to hundreds of hours of Beatles recordings. Revisiting them after 25 years reminded him of the fun they'd had creating those songs, and since he wasn't obligated to make a new album just yet, his random sessions were pressure-free. His next release, 1997's *Flaming Pie*, was recorded sporadically as opportunity and inspiration struck.

"Young Boy" was performed entirely by Paul and Steve Miller. The two had met in the late '60s when Miller was recording at the same studio as the Beatles. Paul played drums on Miller's "My Dark Hour" and the two stayed in touch. Paul's teenage son James had been riffling through his dad's record collection when he came across the Miller album *Brave New World* and heard the song, which inspired Paul to give Miller a ring and ask if he'd like to work on some music together.

"Young Boy", recorded at Miller's studio in Sun Valley, Idaho, was partially inspired by Paul's son, although Paul adds that it's really for anyone looking for love and wondering which person amidst the billions on the planet is the best match for them.

Originally titled "Poor Boy", Paul wrote the song in the three hours it took for Linda to prepare a vegetarian meal at the Long Island home of chef Pierre Franey. It was only after Paul finished that he realized a girl had been lying on a nearby couch the entire time.

"Young Boy" was featured in the soundtrack of the 1997 comedy *Fathers' Day* starring Robin Williams and Billy Crystal.

Paul McCartney – vocals, acoustic guitar, bass, Hammond organ, drums
Steve Miller – lead guitar, rhythm guitar

155. BEAUTIFUL NIGHT
Paul McCartney

Written by Paul McCartney
Recorded May 13-14, 1996
Released December 15, 1997
Album: FLAMING PIE

After the 1995 sessions for "Real Love", Ringo said he enjoyed recording at Paul's home studio in Sussex and that they should do it again sometime. To that end, Paul decided to purchase an exact replica of Ringo's drum kit and installed it at his studio. In May 1996, they reunited for "Beautiful Night", a song Paul had written ten years earlier.

Although he had recorded several versions of the song previously, he was never satisfied. He changed a few lyrics and added an uptempo ending, and this version, featuring lush orchestration by George Martin, was the charm. Paul said recording with Ringo was like the old days again. During the fadeout, the two are heard laughing and exchanging friendly banter.

A love song that forsakes chasing dreams and castles in the sky in favor of simply enjoying each other on a "beautiful night," the lyrics mention getting "a medal from a local neighborhood". On March 11, 1997, Paul became Sir Paul McCartney when he was knighted by Queen Elizabeth II at Buckingham Palace. When Ringo and George heard about it, they dubbed him "Your Holiness."

"Beautiful Night" was the final single released from *Flaming Pie* (an album named after John Lennon's facetious story of how the Beatles got their name—from a man who appeared "on a flaming pie"). It was also the last single Linda McCartney sang backup on before her death.

Paul McCartney – vocals, piano, Hammond organ, electric guitar,
    bass, percussion
Linda McCartney – backing vocals
Ringo Starr – drums, backing vocals
Jeff Lynne – electric guitar, acoustic guitar, backing vocals

156. LA DE DA
Ringo Starr

Written by Richard Starkey, Mark Hudson, Dean Grakal and Steve
 Dudas
Recorded September 29, 1997
Released June 1, 1998
Album: VERTICAL MAN

In the six years since Ringo's last studio album, he lived up to his
commitment to adopt a healthier lifestyle, even becoming a
vegetarian like Paul and George. His wife Barbara left acting to
focus on charity work and established a free clinic for addiction
recovery.

Ringo's 1998 album *Vertical Man* mirrored his own victory
through songs such as "La De Da", a singalong about not letting life
defeat you. Backing vocals included Ringo's wife, his daughter Lee,
and over three dozen friends and relatives.

Vertical Man was chosen as the album title after Ringo came
across a quote in a book that Barbara's daughter Francesca brought
home. Poet Wystan Hugh Auden wrote, "Let's hear it for the
vertical man, so much praise is given to the horizontal one."
Realizing how close he had come to making himself "horizontal"
(that is, dead), Ringo vowed to live his life "vertically" and
encourage others to do the same.

The positive example of a now-sober Starr has been credited for
saving the lives of more than one bandmate who had been on the
same road to ruin he had traveled.

Ringo Starr – vocals, drums, percussion, bongos
Paul McCartney – bass, backing vocals
Joe Walsh – electric guitar, slide guitar, backing vocals
Mark Hudson – electric guitar, acoustic guitar, backing vocals
Steve Dudas – electric guitar, acoustic guitar
Jim Cox – B3 organ
Barbara Bach Starkey, Lee Starkey, Mark Hudson, Sarah Hudson,
 Keith Allison, Nils Lofgrin, others – backing vocals

157. THE KING OF BROKEN HEARTS
Ringo Starr

Written by Richard Starkey, Mark Hudson, Dean Grakal and Steve
   Dudas
Recorded February 1997–February 1998
Released 1998
Album: VERTICAL MAN

Not to be confused with a George Strait song of the same name,
"The King of Broken Hearts" was one of eleven songs co-written by
Ringo for his 1998 album *Vertical Man*.

As he had begun doing on *Time Takes Time*, he was putting more
of himself in the songs he chose to write. As he told *Billboard*
magazine, "Before, I'd just sort of pick out songs other people had
written that I thought were vaguely trying to say what I would have
liked to say. On this, we're really trying to say what I want to say,
thank you."

Ringo had hoped to include George Harrison on the song, but
George wasn't in the mood and declined. A couple of weeks later,
Ringo called him just to say hello and George was playing a dobro.
Ringo exclaimed that a dobro would sound great on "The King of
Broken Hearts" and George finally consented. Tapes were
exchanged and George sent back overdubs that made Ringo cry
with joy. "Every note he plays is just the right one," Ringo said.
"The emotion never fails to raise goosebumps on my neck."

Adding an additional Beatles touch to this tune about losing at
love was a Strawberry Fields-style flute part played on the Mellotron
by producer Mark Hudson.

Ringo Starr – vocals, drums, percussion
George Harrison – slide guitar
Mark Hudson – guitar, bass, keyboards, Mellotron, percussion,
   backing vocals
Steve Dudas – acoustic guitar, electric guitar
Jim Cox – electric piano
John Baxter – pedal steel guitar

158. ONE
Ringo Starr

Written by Richard Starkey, Mark Hudson, Dean Grakal and Steve
  Dudas
Recorded February 1997–February 1998
Released 1998
Album: VERTICAL MAN

Ringo met songwriter Dean Grakal at a New Year's Eve party in
1996. Grakal suggested they write some songs together with Mark
Hudson, a producer who had worked with Cher, Aerosmith and
Hanson. Hudson's initial rise to fame was as a member of the
Hudson Brothers, who had hits in the 1970s with "So You Are a
Star" and "Rendezvous".

Their alliance turned out to be a good one, as Hudson would
become Ringo's producer for his next few albums. Along with
guitarist Steve Dudas, the foursome would write many songs
together and be affectionately known by Ringo as the Roundheads.
Among their first collaborations was the single "One", about a
lonely man left behind by his "one girl."

The entire album *Vertical Man* was recorded at Hudson's humble
studio located above a Thai restaurant in Los Angeles. More than
once, the owners downstairs interrupted sessions by coming up to
complain about the noise or to collect the rent. They were
sometimes appeased by being invited to participate in a session.

The open-door policy likewise applied to any musician who
dropped by to say hello. Among those visiting were Steven Tyler,
Alanis Morrisette and Tom Petty, who all appeared on the album.

Ringo Starr – vocals, drums, bongos, percussion
Mark Hudson – electric guitar, acoustic guitar, keyboards, backing
  vocals
Steve Dudas – bass guitar, electric guitar
Jim Cox – B3 organ
John Baxter – pedal steel guitar
Scott Gordon – harmonica, percussion

159. FLUID
The Fireman (Paul McCartney and Youth)

Written by Paul McCartney
Recorded February 1988
Released September 6, 1998
Album: RUSHES

For The Fireman's second go-round, Paul and techno remix artist Youth referenced "Penny Lane" by titling the album *Rushes*, as in "the fireman rushes in from the pouring rain; very strange."

Indeed, *Rushes* made for another very strange collection by the collaborators of *Strawberry Oceans Ship Forest*, only with more variety this time, culling samples from unreleased tracks and original riffs created expressly for the project rather than lingering on one musical theme. Youth was much happier with *Rushes*, as were critics.

The promo single "Fluid" is the hypnotic weaving of a repeating piano statement and a countering melody of high notes played on a bass guitar. The sound effects of ocean waves, indistinguishable voices, and a woman sensuously moaning "Oh yeah" give the melancholy melody an added element of intrigue.

Making experimental music behind the façade of The Fireman gave Paul the freedom to create calculated chaos outside of the parameters he was expected to cater to. As far back as *Sgt. Pepper*, he had made many tape loop-based mashups. He once told John he was thinking of putting it all out on an album called *Paul McCartney Goes Too Far*.

Despite most fans already being aware of who was at the center of the circle, Paul enjoyed milking the ruse to the point of hosting an online Q&A as The Fireman, wearing a ski mask, dark glasses and a yellow rain hat as he played cuts from the album. He didn't speak on the webcast, instead having a young girl read his evasive answers to the questions submitted: "What inspired this album?" "Night skies, flowing streams and whipped cream fire extinguishers."

Paul McCartney – piano, keyboards, bass, electric guitar, drums,
   percussion

160. WIDE PRAIRIE
Linda McCartney

Written by Linda McCartney
Recorded November 15, 1973
Released November 9, 1998
Album: WIDE PRAIRIE

In the mid-'90s, a fan wrote to Linda to say she had enjoyed "Seaside Woman" and wanted to know if there were any unreleased songs she had done. Prior to her death from breast and liver cancer at age 56, Linda planned to compile all of the music she had recorded with Paul over the previous 25 years. Following her death on April 17, 1998, Paul completed the project as a tribute to his partner of three decades and released it that fall as she had intended.

Linda wrote the playful title song—"Wide Prairie"—from the mostly fictitious perspective of a life spent riding horses on the prairies of Arizona and "feeling perky" in Albuquerque (a line changed from the original "eating jerky", no longer appropriate for the vegetarian). Linda had attended the University of Arizona and loved horses all her life. The very week she died, she enjoyed a horseback ride.

Linda's spoken intro to "Wide Prairie" makes mention of Paris, where she and Wings recorded the song in 1973 (in the same studio where the Beatles had recorded "Can't Buy Me Love"). Her tongue-in-cheek vocals twang out an exaggerated Western accent that was reminiscent of "Man We Was Lonely" from Paul's first solo album.

Linda McCartney – vocals, electric piano
Paul McCartney – piano, bass, electric piano, organ, backing vocals
Denny Laine – acoustic guitar
Jimmy McCulloch – electric guitar
Davey Lutton – drums
Vassar Clements – fiddle
Hewlett Quillen – trombone
William Puett, Thaddeus Richard, Norman Ray – saxophones
George Tidwell and Barry McDonald – trumpets

161. THE LIGHT COMES FROM WITHIN
Linda McCartney

Written by Linda and Paul McCartney
Recorded March 18, 1998
Released January 25, 1999
Album: WIDE PRAIRIE

In 1998, the McCartneys recorded three new compositions that became a part of Linda's posthumous album *Wide Prairie*. "Appaloosa" was her tribute to the Indian tribe known for breeding stallions in the old Northwest (Linda herself owned a beloved Appaloosa named Blankit). "Cow" eulogized trusting cattle destined for slaughter.

The third new song, released as a single, was Linda's biting rebuke to critics who had never accepted her. Over the years, she endured jealousy for marrying Paul, ridicule in being considered a "hick", and mockery for her musical ability in Wings. In terms of having been on the receiving end of condemnation in connection with the Beatles, she was second only to Yoko.

Those who roundly dismissed Linda McCartney failed to take into account her achievements. Aside from accomplishments as an animal rights activist, she created a popular line of vegetarian frozen meals, which made her wealthy independent of Paul. In 1968, before the world had heard of Annie Leibovitz, Linda had been the first female photographer whose work appeared on the cover of *Rolling Stone*. Her photos of rock stars are considered among the best, and during her lifetime she amassed a collection of 200,000 images, many of which have been exhibited in galleries worldwide.

Telling her critics that "oppression won't win" and "the light comes from within" (with a couple of expletives thrown in), Linda had the last word on this, her final studio recording before her death. Only Paul and their son James perform with her.

Linda McCartney – vocals, electric piano
Paul McCartney – bass, pianos, organ, drums, backing vocals
James McCartney – electric guitar, acoustic guitar

162. NO OTHER BABY
Paul McCartney

Written by Dickie Bishop and Bob Watson
Recorded March 5, 1999
Released October 24, 1999
Album: RUN DEVIL RUN

Following Linda's 1998 death, Paul decried the standard advice often given to the grieving to stay busy. Although he participated in various tributes to his late wife, he allowed himself the freedom to step away from recording for almost a year in a respectable mourning period.

In March 1999, Paul rented Abbey Road Studio 2 for an oldies project Linda had urged him to do for some time. *Run Devil Run* was a collection of mostly covers, an album of songs that would take him back to his roots. Unlike the familiar classics on John Lennon's *Rock 'n' Roll* album, Paul chose more obscure songs he had liked as a teenager. During the recording process, he was pleased that his musicians—which included members of Pink Floyd and Deep Purple—were unfamiliar with the originals, meaning that they could contribute a fresh approach to the decades-old material.

The single "No Other Baby" was first recorded in 1957 by Dickie Bishop and the Sidekicks, though Paul was more familiar with a 1958 remake by a British group whose name he couldn't remember. When he asked George Martin if he happened to know who they were, it turned out to be The Vipers, and their recording was one that Martin himself had produced.

A promotional video for "No Other Baby" showed Paul in a rowboat singing, playing guitar and sleeping, undisturbed by circling sharks, icebergs and storms.

Paul McCartney – vocals, electric guitar, bass
David Gilmour – electric guitar, backing vocals
Mick Green – electric guitar
Pete Wingfield – Hammond organ
Ian Paice – drums

163. RUN DEVIL RUN
Paul McCartney

Written by Paul McCartney
Recorded March 3, 1999
Released October 1999
Album: RUN DEVIL RUN

Having grown up in a uniquely creative environment, all of Paul's children became artists or musicians. In 1999 his adopted daughter Heather launched a line of designer pottery and home goods known as the Heather McCartney Houseware Collection. Paul went to Atlanta that January to help promote Heather's work at a trade show. Joining them was Paul's 21-year-old James, who wanted to explore what Paul referred to as the "funky" side of Atlanta.

While giving their regards to Broad Street, they came upon Miller's Rexall Drugs. Like the famed A. Schwab on Memphis' Beale Street, the store's quirky merchandise included a section of voodoo potions and remedies. Looking in the shop window, Paul spotted a bottle of bath salts bearing the name "Run Devil Run".

Recognizing immediately that it made an interesting song title, Paul said lyrics easily followed: "Run Devil Run, the angels having fun, making winners out of sinners, better leave before it's done." Released as a single, the Little Richard-style song became the title track of his homage to '50s rock and roll. A somewhat doctored photo of Miller's Rexall Drugs (now relocated to Decatur, Georgia) adorns the cover of *Run Devil Run.*

As for the bath salts, Paul said he would be bathing with them, not because he thought he had demons to get rid of, "but there may be one or two lurking, and this stuff is definitely going to do the trick."

Paul McCartney – vocals, bass
David Gilmour – electric guitar, lap steel guitar
Mick Green – electric guitar
Pete Wingfield – piano
Ian Paice – drums

164. COME ON CHRISTMAS, CHRISTMAS COME ON
Ringo Starr

Written by Richard Starkey, Mark Hudson and Dean Grakal
Recorded 1999
Released October 19, 1999
Album: I WANNA BE SANTA CLAUS

Following John's "Happy Xmas (War is Over)", Paul's "Wonderful Christmastime" and George's "Ding Dong, Ding Dong", Ringo was the last of the ex-Beatles to issue a solo Christmas single but the only one to release an entire album of holiday fare.

A collection of yuletide standards and new songs co-written by Ringo (some composed in the summer of 1998), *I Wanna Be Santa Claus* included a remake of "Christmas Time (Is Here Again)", first recorded by the Beatles for their fan club in 1967.

Like most of the songs on Ringo's previous album *Vertical Man*, *I Wanna Be Santa Claus* was co-written with Mark Hudson. Over the course of what would become a ten-year alliance, he and Ringo collaborated on 64 songs.

Ringo always felt that on the early Beatles albums, his bass drum was too low in the mix. So this time, he told engineer Scott Gordon that he wanted the "kick drum of death." With a gigantic thumping beat that would make Gary Glitter proud, "Come on Christmas, Christmas Come On" was given enough bottom end to rattle the North Pole.

In his opening command, "A bit more 51," Ringo was instructing the control booth to turn up the echo on his voice, "51" being a setting on their Alesis effects panel.

Ringo Starr – vocals, drums, percussion
Mark Hudson – electric guitar, bass, backing vocals
Scott Gordon – harmonica, percussion
Pat Zicari – saxophone
Gary Burr, Sarah Hudson, Brett Hudson, Steffan Fantini, Marc
    Fantini, Kiley Oliver, Tess Whiteheart, Dick Monda, the Xmas
    Files Singers – backing vocals

165. VO!CE
Heather Mills

Written by Nikki Patrelakis, Heather Mills, Paul McCartney
Recorded November 1999
Released December 13, 1999
Album: VO!CE CD single

Heather Mills had a bumpy childhood that saw her running away from home at 15 and getting arrested for stealing jewelry. She grew up to be a model and, later, an award-winning activist who created a charity to provide artificial limbs to amputee victims of war in Bosnia. She herself lost a leg at age 25 after being struck by a motorcycle.

Paul met Heather on May 20, 1999 at the Pride of Britain Awards, where Paul was to present the Linda McCartney Award for Animal Welfare. Heather was also a presenter, and Paul was impressed with her speech and her humanitarian work to the point of making the biggest donation her charity had ever seen.

Later that year, Heather asked Paul to participate in a fundraising CD called "VO!CE". The resulting single was a narrative piece about giving voice to the disabled, scripted and spoken by Heather. Over its techno music track—created by electronica jazz composer Nikko Patrelakis—Paul sang phrases like "Why don't you ask her? She has a voice." Royalties went to the Heather Mills Health Trust.

In 2000, Paul attended Heather's 32nd birthday party, and by February 2001 the two would become close enough to take a ten-day tropical vacation together in the West Indies. They announced their engagement that summer and were married the following year on June 11, 2002, a week before Paul's 60th birthday. Unlike his first marriage to Linda at a London registrar's office, the wedding took place at a 17th century castle in Ireland with 300 guests in attendance.

Heather Mills – narration
Paul McCartney – backing vocals
Jonathan Elvey – piano
Stamon Semsis – violas

166. FREE NOW
Paul McCartney

Written by Paul McCartney
Recorded 2000
Released August 21, 2000
Album: LIVERPOOL SOUND COLLAGE

Although John Lennon was thought of as the avant-garde Beatle, Paul introduced his bandmates to experimental composition long before Yoko brought her bed-ins and bagism. Pioneered in the 1950s, the genre known as musique concrète particularly fascinated Paul. This style of composing—by piecing together sound snippets—is best known to Beatle fans via "Revolution 9".

Even before the White Album, however, Paul orchestrated what is possibly the rarest of all Beatle recordings, "Carnival of Light". Created for and publicly played only at a 1967 "happening" for artist friends of Paul, the bizarre sound collage is fourteen minutes of random instruments, sound effects, and John yelling, "Barcelona!" George Harrison hated "Carnival of Light" so much that he vetoed including it on the *Beatles Anthology* CDs, so it remains unreleased in any form. The infamous track is so in demand that fans have resorted to posting fake versions of it on YouTube.

It's unlikely that George thought much of Paul's only 2000 release, *Liverpool Sound Collage*. Forsaking his Fireman persona, Paul openly indulged in an album of musique concrète after being asked by artist and friend Peter Blake to provide a soundtrack for his latest exhibition.

To create *Liverpool Sound Collage*, Paul gathered recordings of traffic, pedestrians and other local sounds. Reuniting with Youth and working with mixmasters from the group Super Furry Animals, Paul blended in snippets from his classical works as well as dialogue from vintage Beatle sessions. By means of a 1965 clip, the voice of George Harrison introduces the single "Free Now".

Paul McCartney – voices, various instruments
John Lennon, George Harrison, Ringo Starr – voices

167. FROM A LOVER TO A FRIEND
Paul McCartney

Written by Paul McCartney
Recorded February 20, 2001
Released October 29, 2001
Album: DRIVING RAIN

A long break from traditional musicmaking saw Paul indulging in painting and poetry, attending gallery showings of his artwork, and publishing a collection of his writings called *Blackbird Singing*. He also took part in charity events and visited George in Milan, Italy.

Finally returning to the studio in 2001, Paul sought the same spontaneous spirit he had achieved during 1999's *Run Devil Run* sessions. Relying on a fresh lineup of studio musicians suggested by producer David Kahne (The Bangles, Stevie Nicks, Kelly Clarkson and others), Paul once again demoed each new song for the band and allowed only a modicum of rehearsal before committing to live capture.

The first single from these Los Angeles sessions, "From a Lover to a Friend", was written late at night at Paul's London home. Noodling with two song fragments previously written but unrelated, lyrics began to form almost subconsciously to create a revealing monologue that took even Paul by surprise. The solemn song speaks of having a dilemma and being "duty bound" to reveal the truth when the time comes. In the chorus, he asks permission to let him love again. It's unclear whether he's asking Linda, Heather Mills, or himself.

Only a few months prior, *Now* magazine reported that Paul still "talks" to Linda. Regarding his new relationship with Heather, he said Linda would likely tell him, "If I was there, you'd be dead meat, sucker. But I'm not and I want you to be happy."

Paul McCartney – vocals, piano, bass
Rusty Anderson – 12-string electric guitar
Gabe Dixon – keyboards
Abe Laboriel, Jr. – drums

168. FREEDOM
Paul McCartney

Written by Paul McCartney
Recorded October 20, 2001
Released November 5, 2001
Album: DRIVING RAIN

Paul and his then-fiancée Heather spent the second week of September 2001 in New York, attending award ceremonies and watching a men's tennis match. They were scheduled to head back the morning of September 11th and were already on the airplane at JFK when the World Trade Center was attacked by terrorists. To the right of the runway Paul could see smoke billowing from the Twin Towers. He thought it was an optical illusion until a steward told him something serious was happening and led him off the plane.

Six weeks after the attack, Paul organized a benefit concert at Madison Square Garden to honor first responders and to raise funds for the families of firefighters and policemen who perished. The Concert for New York City included performances by Elton John, The Who, James Taylor, Billy Joel and many others, plus short films by Woody Allen and Martin Scorcese. In all, over 60 celebrities took part. The concert raised $35 million, and Paul also wrote anonymous checks to some of the first responders to help them with medical expenses. His own father Jim had served as a fireman in WWII.

Closing out the 5½ hour event, Paul debuted a song he wrote for the occasion, "Freedom", a defiant anthem about fighting for the right to be free. The song came to him after watching a speech by President Bush regarding the attacks. In interviews, Paul—a well-known pacifist—supported a U.S. response, saying that sometimes there is no choice but to fight back, and this was one of those times.

Paul McCartney – vocals, guitars, bass
Eric Clapton – electric guitar
Rusty Anderson – electric guitar
Gabe Dixon – electric piano
Abe Laboriel, Jr. – drums

169. YOUR LOVING FLAME
Paul McCartney

Written by Paul McCartney
Recorded June 19, 2001
Released June 24, 2002
Album: DRIVING RAIN

Paul wrote the romantic ballad "Your Loving Flame" in a 31st floor suite at the luxurious Carlyle Hotel in New York, built in 1930. Soaking up the rich history and enjoying a stunning view of Central Park through a plate glass window, Paul felt as if he were transported back to the days of Cole Porter. Luckily, there was a Steinway baby grand piano in the room that allowed him to channel his inner Porter. The song came together in about an hour.

The last track recorded for *Driving Rain*, "Your Loving Flame" was the first song Paul had written with Heather Mills in mind. Pondering the uncertainties of new love and questioning whether both parties feel the same way, the one thing clear to him is that she could be the one to chase his blues away. He called Heather to play it for her as soon as he finished writing it.

Driving Rain contains other songs linked to Heather ("About You", "Heather") and at least one song written during his mourning period for Linda ("Magic"). The latter was an uplifting recollection of the night he and Linda met at the Bag O' Nails in London. Introducing himself to her before she left the club had been life-changing "magic."

Paul McCartney – vocals, piano, bass, tambourine
Rusty Anderson – acoustic guitar, electric guitar, backing vocals
Gabe Dixon – Hammond organ, backing vocals
Abe Laboriel, Jr. – drums, backing vocals
David Kahne – sampled strings
David Campbell – viola
Matt Funes – viola
Joel Derouin – violin
Larry Corbett – cello

170. VANILLA SKY
Paul McCartney

Written by Paul McCartney
Recorded June 2001
Released December 4, 2001
Album: VANILLA SKY (soundtrack)

During the Los Angeles sessions for *Driving Rain*, Paul was approached by director Cameron Crowe (*Jerry Maguire, Almost Famous*) to write a song for his new movie, an English adaptation of a Spanish psychological thriller originally titled *Open Your Eyes*.

After watching a 40-minute edit starring Tom Cruise and Penélope Cruz (who also acted in the Spanish version), Paul played Crowe some tracks he had recorded, but Crowe felt something more low-key was needed to soothe audiences at the end of the mind-bending movie.

The film's English title, *Vanilla Sky*, lent itself well to rhymes which came together quickly. The opening line of the song ("The chef prepares a special menu for your delight, oh my") was inspired while Paul was at dinner. Before the first course, he was presented with something he hadn't ordered which the waiter identified as an "amuse-bouche" (French for a complimentary appetizer to prepare the palate). Paul said he was tempted to make "The chef prepares an amuse-bouche" the opening line but knew it would be lost on most listeners, if he were even able to pronounce it.

He wrote the essence of the song in ten minutes, completed it in three days, and delivered the recording of "Vanilla Sky" in a week. He told Crowe, "If you don't like it, I'll call it 'Manila Envelope'." Crowe did like it and it went on to win the Critic's Choice Movie Award for Best Song. "Vanilla Sky" was also nominated for a Grammy, a Golden Globe, and an Oscar.

The film's actual music score, as surreal as the film itself, was created by Heart's Nancy Wilson, Crowe's wife at the time.

Paul McCartney – vocals, guitars, percussion
Jim Walker – flute

171. DRIVING RAIN
Paul McCartney

Written by Paul McCartney
Recorded February 27, 2001
Released November 12, 2001
Album: DRIVING RAIN

A lot of California rain accompanied Paul's February 2001 sessions in L.A. On one of the nicer days, he went for a drive in a little Corvette, exploring the Pacific Coast Highway and stopping for lunch in Malibu. After his pleasant day off, he felt like writing a song inspired by his road trip. Starting out that night as a piano ballad, "Driving Rain" evolved into one of the more driven numbers on the new album.

The first verse took a cue from the Los Angeles house Paul was renting. The security system had a malfunction that kept an error message on the monitor saying "Something's open." Even with all the doors and windows closed and locked, the LED would continue to insist that something was open. "Not very reassuring," said Paul. He found it comical and used the error message to his advantage via the line, "Something's open, it's my heart."

Turning random observations like that into songs, Paul said, is really the same approach a good photographer uses. He recalled that Linda was always on the lookout for the most interesting moment to shoot. "You just have to be open [to it]."

Released as a single in Japan, "Driving Rain" became the title track for the album, which was originally to be titled *Blue Skies* but was changed just prior to release. The grainy black and white album cover photo was a selfie Paul had taken in a bathroom with his new toy, a Casio Wrist Camera watch.

Paul McCartney – vocals, acoustic guitar, bass
Rusty Anderson – 12-string electric guitar
Gabe Dixon – electric piano
David Kahne – synthesizer
Abe Laboriel, Jr. – drums

172. LONELY ROAD
Paul McCartney

Written by Paul McCartney
Recorded February 16, 2001
Released November 12, 2001
Album: DRIVING RAIN

Soon after Heather Mills' birthday in January 2001, she and Paul vacationed in India, where Paul bought her an engagement ring to the tune of £15,000. One afternoon at their hotel he wrote what would become the opening track on *Driving Rain*.

"Lonely Road" begins with a simple and steady bass riff, conjuring images of white lines rolling by in the middle of a highway. The arrangement builds gradually into an angry rocker about not getting hurt again. Paul's raspy vocal was partly intentional but mostly unavoidable as he had lost his voice days earlier after a shouting match with an Indian merchant. Paul had been sold a carpet that he was assured was one of a kind. He discovered twenty identical carpets for sale in the next town.

Paul wrote "Lonely Road" in about an hour and called it a defiant song against loneliness. Trying to get over someone, trying something new, and going somewhere old in search of a pot of gold had direct correlations to his trip to India with Heather, though he added that it's symbolic for anyone who's been through any sort of struggle.

In the music video, a barefoot Paul is dressed as an auto mechanic (his shirt says "Affordable Mufflers and Brakes"). He drives a red convertible down a desert highway, refusing to pick up a string of hitchhiking harlots. One of them retaliates by slamming a Hofner bass around in the sagebrush.

Paul McCartney – vocals, guitars, bass
Rusty Anderson – guitars, pedal steel guitar
Gabe Dixon – electric piano
David Kahne – organ
Abe Laboriel, Jr. – drums, tambourine

173. RINSE THE RAINDROPS
Paul McCartney

Written by Paul McCartney
Recorded February 19, 2001
Released 2002
Album: DRIVING RAIN

Rarely does Paul write lyrics first and music later. One of the few examples was "All My Loving", the words of which were written on a tour bus on the way to a gig. When words alone do come to him, they tend to remain in the form of poetry. Many of these words in search of music were published in 2001's *Blackbird Singing: Poems and Lyrics, 1965-1999*.

On a sailing trip, some words came together for Paul and he wasn't certain whether they should be a poem or a song. Having come up with a rough melody, he demoed "Rinse the Raindrops" on an acoustic guitar for his *Driving Rain* musicians and then had them jam live while he played bass and sang.

Thirty minutes later, they had recorded a half dozen rocking variations on the theme, with Paul singing the two verses an estimated 48 times in as many possible ways as he could think of. That night, after everyone left, producer David Kahne stayed at the studio till 4 a.m. editing the best parts down to a more manageable length.

With a voice still raw from chewing out a corrupt carpet dealer, the wildest McCartney yell of all time can be heard at 9:22 in the 10-minute album mix. Other mixes of "Rinse the Raindrops" would follow, including a shorter single specifically for juke boxes.

The lyrics, consistent with the theme that runs through *Driving Rain*, focus on clearing one's head and breaking through the ice in order to awaken and see the sunshine again.

Paul McCartney – vocals, bass, Spanish guitar
Rusty Anderson – electric guitar
Gabe Dixon – electric piano, Hammond organ, piano
Abe Laboriel, Jr. – drums, accordion

174. HELLO GOODBYE (LIVE)
Paul McCartney

Written by Paul McCartney and John Lennon
Recorded May 1, 2002
Released November 11, 2002
Album: BACK IN THE U.S.

In 2002, Paul's Driving USA tour was his first in nine years and his first following the deaths of Linda and George Harrison. The tour featured the new band members he had worked with on *Driving Rain* plus the return of "Wix" Wickens, who had played keyboards on his previous two tours. He has used this touring lineup ever since.

Originally recorded by the Beatles in 1967, "Hello Goodbye" was their first single release after the death of manager Brian Epstein. The Beatles' right-hand man and Epstein's assistant Alistair Taylor said he was at Paul's home in London when Paul offered to show him how easy it was to write a song. Sitting at a harmonium, Paul instructed Taylor to shout out the opposite of anything Paul said. The resulting hello/goodbye, high/low, up/down, stop/go, etc. would trigger this song which became part of *Magical Mystery Tour*. Paul said that even though it's about duality, he is advocating the practical outlook that you can't have one without the other.

John considered the song (originally titled "Hello Hello") a throwaway, but liked the upbeat ending tagged on it. The official lyrics over that coda are "Hela Heba Helloa", nonsense words presumed to combine "hello," "aloha," and "haere ra" (Māori for "goodbye").

"Hello Goodbye" opened all of Paul's 2002 shows. Its performance at The Palace of Auburn Hills in Detroit was issued as a single to promote his live concert album *Back in the U.S.*

Paul McCartney – vocals, bass
Rusty Anderson – electric guitar, backing vocals
Brian Ray – electric guitar, backing vocals
Paul "Wix" Wickens – keyboards
Abe Laboriel, Jr. – drums

175. STUCK INSIDE A CLOUD
George Harrison

Written by George Harrison
Recorded 1999
Released November 18, 2002
Album: BRAINWASHED

When George wasn't making music, he indulged in what had become his pride and joy, gardening at his Friar Park estate. It was while tending to his grounds in 1997 that he noticed a lump in his throat. Diagnosed with cancer, he attributed it to a lifetime of smoking. Following surgery and radiation treatment, he was given an all-clear. By 2001, however, he developed lung cancer followed by a malignant brain tumor.

George had begun working on a final album, to be punningly titled *Portrait of a Leg End*. This collection of new and existing material, recorded with his son Dhani and drummer Jim Keltner, only made it to the demo stage before George's death on November 29, 2001. The unfinished songs included "Stuck Inside a Cloud".

A few months later, Dhani and Jeff Lynne set about to complete the album at Lynne's studio. George had left copious notes to guide the post-production process. Among his instructions was that the songs not become "too posh" (in this case, "overproduced," a directive aimed at Lynne).

The lyrics of "Stuck Inside a Cloud" reflect George's waning state in which he was ready to leave his failing body and touch the "lotus feet" sacred to his Hindu beliefs. It was Dhani's favorite song on the album, prompting him to make it the seventh track. Like John's magical number nine, George felt the number seven had a recurring significance in his life. "Stuck Inside a Cloud" was released as a radio single to promote George's final album, titled *Brainwashed*.

George Harrison – vocals, acoustic guitar, slide guitar
Jeff Lynne – bass, piano, electric guitar
Dhani Harrison – organ
Jim Keltner – drums

176. NEVER WITHOUT YOU
Ringo Starr

Written by Richard Starkey, Mark Hudson and Gary Nicholson
Recorded 2002
Released February 17, 2003
Album: RINGO RAMA

In late 2001, both George Harrison and Ringo's daughter Lee Starkey were fighting brain cancer. The last time Ringo saw George was in Switzerland, where George had relocated during the final months of his life. At the end of their visit, Ringo mentioned that he had to head to Boston for his daughter's surgery. In characteristic good humor, a bedridden George offered, "Do you want me to come with you?"

Lee Starkey survived her cancer and is alive and well today. George lost his battle at the age of 58 on November 29, 2001 with Olivia and Dhani by his side.

Of all the Beatles, Ringo had remained the closest to George. In early 2002, Ringo wanted to do a song in honor of both George and John as well as his close friend Harry Nilsson, who died of a heart attack a few years earlier. Country songwriter Gary Nicholson had written a song that Ringo could adapt, but trying to gear it toward all three of his fallen friends made it a bit busy. Rather than becoming an "Abraham, Martin and John" clone, Ringo's final product, "Never Without You", focused specifically on George.

With mentions of "Here Comes the Sun", "Within You Without You" and "All Things Must Pass", this single from *Ringo Rama* has Eric Clapton playing slide guitar in George's trademark style.

Ringo Starr – vocals, keyboards, drums, percussion
Eric Clapton – lead guitar solo
Mark Hudson – bass, backing vocals
Gary Burr – acoustic guitar, backing vocals
Gary Nicholson – 12-string acoustic guitar
Steve Dudas – electric guitar
Jim Cox – organ

177. IMAGINE ME THERE
Ringo Starr

Written by Richard Starkey, Mark Hudson and Gary Burr
Recorded 2002
Released March 25, 2003
Album: RINGO RAMA

While "Never Without You" became Ringo's tribute to George, he managed to slide in references to John Lennon and Harry Nilsson elsewhere on *Ringo Rama*. At the end of "Missouri Loves Company", a banjo reminiscent of Nilsson's "Everybody's Talkin'" is joined by a barely audible "We love You, Harry." Ringo's nod to John, meanwhile, is the promo single "Imagine Me There".

A song of encouragement and support, there is no direct reference to John other than having "Imagine" in the title. But the orchestration has a decided "Dear Prudence" vibe to it in addition to other Lennon characteristics.

Already in the studio to do the guitar solo for "Never Without You", Eric Clapton played another for "Imagine Me There".

Guest performing as well was renowned jazz bassist Charlie Haden. Co-writer Gary Burr, one of Nashville's most successful country music songwriters, felt that Haden's inventive choice of notes gave the ballad too flamboyant of a treatment. Ringo, however, was quite pleased with it. Burr, a non-drinker, was so dismayed to the point of resorting to a Smirnoff. But he came to appreciate the bass track, and he now admits it's his favorite part of the song.

Ringo Starr – vocals, electric guitar, drums, percussion
Eric Clapton – lead guitar solo
Mark Hudson – keyboards, bass, backing vocals
Gary Burr – acoustic guitar, backing vocals
Jim Cox – piano
Steve Dudas – electric guitar
Charlie Haden – upright bass
Dan Higgins – flute

178. ANY ROAD
George Harrison

Written by George Harrison
Recorded 2001
Released May 12, 2003
Album: BRAINWASHED

Written as far back as 1988, "Any Road" was one of the demos George recorded in 2001 and bequeathed to Dhani and Jeff Lynne to finish. With a jaunty journeyman's mentality, this opening track of *Brainwashed* would have fit right in with the Traveling Wilburys catalog.

The main idea behind the rollicking tongue-in-cheek road song corresponds to a conversation between Alice and the Cheshire Cat in *Alice's Adventures in Wonderland*. Alice is asking for directions but doesn't know her destination. The cat tells her, "Then it doesn't matter which way you go," informing her that she'll get *somewhere*. In "Any Road", George paraphrases, "If you don't know where you're going, any road will take you there."

George felt confident in where he was going in the months prior to his death. Having devoted the better part of his life to mastering the art of dying, he took his impending demise with grace. Among his final intentions were digital reissues of his albums as well as curating a special collection of his Dark Horse era songs and outtakes, the latter of which were posthumously released.

After George's death, his family left a statement which read: "He left this world as he lived in it—conscious of God, fearless of death, and at peace, surrounded by family and friends." His ashes were scattered at a sacred river crossroads in India.

"Any Road" was the only commercially released single from *Brainwashed* and George's last single issued.

George Harrison – vocals, acoustic guitar, slide guitar, banjolele
Jeff Lynne – bass, piano, backing vocals
Dhani Harrison – electric guitar, backing vocals
Jim Keltner – drums

179. TROPIC ISLAND HUM
Paul McCartney

Written by Paul McCartney
Recorded December 14, 1987
Released September 20, 2004
From TROPIC ISLAND HUM (CD single and DVD)

Following the success of 1984's *Rupert and the Frog Song*, Paul reunited with animator Geoff Dunbar and wrote another children's story to be put to film. Paul wanted an animal as the main character, but there were already famous bunnies, mice, chipmunks, pigs and bears populating cartoons, so he landed on a squirrel for the lead.

In *Tropic Island Hum*, a squirrel named Wirral is almost killed when hunters invade his forest. A frog in a hot air balloon helps him escape to a tropic island where other animal refugees celebrate his arrival with this cheerful tribal song. After hearing the plot of the eco-friendly tale, Linda remarked that there was no love interest in the story, so Paul wrote in a sultry squirrel for Wirral to go nuts over. "Boy meets girl with a message," is how Paul described it.

Paul did every one of the many male voices in the cartoon, with Linda providing the spoken voice of the female squirrel, Wilhelmina. Her singing voice was performed by renowned jazz singer Marion Montgomery, whose fans included Frank Sinatra and Nat King Cole. Rounding out the animal chorus was The London Community Gospel Choir. The song and the film's incidental music were scored by George Martin.

The 13-minute cartoon was shown in select theaters preceding Disney's *Hercules* in 1997. In 2004, an edited version of its title song was released as a single in Britain to promote Paul's DVD *The Music and Animation Collection*.

Paul McCartney – vocals, keyboards, bass, upright bass
Linda McCartney – backing vocals
Chris Whitten – drums
Marion Montgomery – backing vocals
London Community Gospel Choir – backing vocals

180. REALLY LOVE YOU
Paul McCartney

Written by Paul McCartney and Richard Starkey
Initially recorded May 14, 1996
Released June 6, 2005
Album: TWIN FREAKS

An impromptu jam session with Paul, Ringo and Jeff Lynne during sessions for *Flaming Pie* in 1996 yielded the first song on which Paul and Ringo shared dual songwriting credit. "Really Love You" is the only song jointly published by Paul's MPL Communications and Ringo's Startling Music.

Having adlibbed his vocals on the spot as a challenge to himself, Paul admits that even he can't explain "I need your heart, Baby, hopping on a plate." Persistent in its beat, Ringo called the finished product "relentless."

Club DJ Roy Kerr (aka the Freelance Hellraiser) gained fame in 2001 as one of the creators of mashups, reinventing songs into new entities. Issued a cease-and-desist order by RCA for an unauthorized mashup involving Christina Aguilera's "Genie in a Bottle", Kerr was ultimately hired by the label to remix her single "Fighter".

Kerr's talents came to the attention of Paul, who hired him to perform 25 minutes of preshow entertainment and join Paul on his 2004 tour in Europe. The radical reworkings of McCartney tracks, often unrecognizable, felt familiar on at least a subliminal level. They were well-received enough for Paul to commission a double album titled *Twin Freaks*. The abstract cover was painted by Paul.

More relentless than ever, its intense and somewhat dark single "Really Love You" also incorporated drum tracks from "What's That You're Doing", Paul's duet with Stevie Wonder from 1982's *Tug of War*. Other tracks on *Twin Freaks* included mashups ranging from Paul's latest album to 1970's "Maybe I'm Amazed".

Paul McCartney – vocals, bass, electric guitar, electric piano
Jeff Lynne – electric guitar, backing vocals
Ringo Starr – drums

181. FADING IN FADING OUT
Ringo Starr

Written by Richard Starkey, Mark Hudson and Gary Burr
Recorded 2004
Released June 7, 2005
Album: CHOOSE LOVE

Ringo's 2005 album *Choose Love* marked his third go-round with The Roundheads, his studio band anchored by Mark Hudson and Gary Burr. Burr, a former member of Pure Prairie League and writer of songs for Juice Newton, The Oak Ridge Boys and Reba McIntyre, co-wrote the album's promotional single, "Fading In Fading Out".

Having lost some of his closest friends in recent years, Ringo's thoughts turned to mortality in this song that focuses on how short life can be. "First you're here, then you're gone, still the world goes on and on," he sings. In ever-encouraging Ringo style, however, the overriding message is that even though we fade in and fade out, we are here right now, and that's what matters. "All we really need is love," he continues, "and when I disappear, I pray that I have left enough."

Each new album meant another tour, and over the years Ringo had found that creating art on his computer was a good way to bide his time in hotel rooms. By 2005 he had accumulated enough digital paintings to hold his first exhibition, titled "My Faces". The pop art images looked straight out of Pepperland, resembling relatives of the Blue Meanies. Ringo's artwork, likened to that of Andy Warhol, continues to sell through auction houses and has been used in a Hard Rock T-shirt collection as well as on Timberland boots.

Ringo Starr – vocals, drums, percussion
Dave Stewart – guitars, backing vocals
Gary Burr – guitars, bass, backing vocals
Robert Randolph – lead guitar
Mark Mirando – electric guitar
Dan Higgins – horns
Gary Grant – horns

182. FINE LINE
Paul McCartney

Written by Paul McCartney
Recorded September 2004
Released August 29, 2005
Album: CHAOS AND CREATION IN THE BACKYARD

George Martin had retired in 1998 after producing his own pet project, *In My Life*, in which hand-picked celebrities such as Robin Williams and Goldie Hawn performed inventive new interpretations of Beatle songs. He returned to the production board only once more in 2006 to oversee the music for Cirque du Soleil's Beatles-themed show *Love*.

Seeking a new producer for his next album, Paul asked for suggestions from Martin, who recommended Nigel Godrich. At first, musical differences of opinion threatened to end the working relationship before it started, with Godrich nixing any of Paul's songs he didn't like. He also insisted that Paul perform the songs by himself rather than rely on the comfortable familiarity of his touring band. The collaboration paid off when the resulting album, *Chaos and Creation in the Backyard*, was nominated for Grammy awards in multiple categories.

One happy accident occurred while creating "Fine Line". Paul hit a wrong note on the bass, but it worked, even complimenting the theme of chaos and creation, so it was kept.

In the bridge of the song, Paul sings, "Come home, brother, all is forgiven." Related or not, the song was recorded the same month that his brother Michael was accused of sexual assault at a family gathering (he was later found not guilty).

"Fine Line" was the first single released from *Chaos and Creation*, the cover of which was a vintage photo of a teenaged Paul playing guitar in the backyard of his childhood home, taken by Michael.

Paul McCartney – vocals, grand piano, spinet piano, electric guitar, acoustic guitar, bass, drums, shakers, tambourine
Millennia Ensemble – strings

183. JENNY WREN
Paul McCartney

Written by Paul McCartney
Recorded October 2004
Released November 21, 2005
Album: CHAOS AND CREATION IN THE BACKYARD

In Charles Dickens' last novel, *Our Mutual Friend*, Jenny Wren was a teenage cripple who looks after her alcoholic father and rises above her challenges. Well-versed in English literature, Paul says it's possible that she was in the far reaches of his mind when he wrote "Jenny Wren", although his unhappy heroine bears more of a resemblance to Eleanor Rigby than to the Dickens dressmaker.

The bulk of "Jenny Wren" was written in a canyon near L.A., where Paul had ventured with his guitar, seeking inspiration from the great outdoors. He finished writing it that evening while dinner was being prepared. Tuning his Epiphone Texan guitar a full step lower as he had done on "Yesterday", Paul played in a finger-picking style similar to "Blackbird".

Being one of Paul's favorite birds, "wren" was a ready name for his fictional femme who takes wing only to meet with the foolish ways of the world but who will sing again one day.

At a 2003 tribute concert for George Harrison, a member of Ravi Shankar's band had played a woodwind instrument called the duduk, an Armenian flute made of apricot wood. Remembering its unique sound, Paul sought out that same musician, Venezuelan flautist Pedro Eustache, to embellish this gentle voice and guitar ballad. Eustache performed his accompaniment in a single take. No additional instruments were added because Paul said he wanted the song to remain intimate, "like two friends playing together."

"Jenny Wren", the second single from *Chaos and Creation in the Backyard,* earned a Grammy nomination for Best Male Pop Vocal Performance.

Paul McCartney – vocals, acoustic guitar, floor tom
Pedro Eustache – duduk

184. THIS NEVER HAPPENED BEFORE
Paul McCartney

Written by Paul McCartney
Recorded November 2003
Released June 2006
Album: CHAOS AND CREATION IN THE BACKYARD

One of Paul's most romantic singles drew its initial inspiration from a distinctive chord sequence Paul liked. "This Never Happened Before" was recorded a month after the birth of Paul and Heather's daughter Beatrice, born October 28, 2003. It had been one of the first songs completed under producer Nigel Godrich and it convinced Paul that the two of them would make a good team.

While getting a massage soon after, Paul played the song for his young masseuse, who remarked that she thought it was magnificent. She mentioned that she was getting married in a few weeks, so Paul sent her a copy of the as-yet-unreleased song to play at her wedding. The couple later wrote Paul back, saying they used the song for their first dance and that their special day went great, filled with laughter and tears. Paul said that sums up what the song is all about for him.

Released as a promotional single to radio stations, "This Never Happened Before" would also provide a sentimental soundtrack for Keanu Reeves and Sandra Bullock to dance to in *The Lake House*.

The single was released in June 2006, the same month Paul turned 64. Despite birthday greetings and bottles of wine, Paul had less than usual to celebrate, as he had separated from Heather just weeks prior. Heather had never gotten along with Paul's adult children, who found her bossy and conniving, but that was only the tip of the iceberg. What had become a contentious partnership was not helped by a media circus that called their marriage "the mistake of the decade."

Paul told the *Daily Mirror* he would be spending his 64th birthday at his farmhouse in Sussex with his daughters Mary and Stella.

Paul McCartney – vocals, grand piano, electric guitar, drums, bass
Millennia Ensemble – strings, brass

185. EVER PRESENT PAST
Paul McCartney

Written by Paul McCartney
Recorded March 2006
Released May 15, 2007
Album: MEMORY ALMOST FULL

When Paul learned that Capitol/EMI, his record distributor for 45 years, was going to take six months to come up with a marketing plan for his 2007 album *Memory Almost Full,* he decided to look for more efficient and modern ways to reach his audience. He left EMI and became the first artist signed to Starbucks' new label Hear Music. The day of the album's release, it was played nonstop in Starbucks' then-15,000 coffee shops worldwide. The in-store promotion accounted for 47% of its first week's sales. *Memory Almost Full* was also Paul's first album to be available as a digital download.

Like many of Paul's songs, "Ever Present Past" began life with as little as a strong opening line. "I've got too much on my plate" struck Paul as a good jumping-off point, inviting him to then explore the causes and effects of someone being too busy. In his case, the overriding specter of superstardom was forefront in his mind. Never in a position to escape his legendary status as a former Beatle, he lyrically alludes to those manic, disorienting years and goes back even further to the things he "thought" he did as a kid.

Originally written as a folksy acoustic guitar tune called "Perfect Lover", "Ever Present Past" received a high-tech treatment in the studio when he reunited with *Driving Rain* producer David Kahne. Despite its wistful theme of time going by too fast, the upbeat song remains optimistic that there is more to be discovered.

A music video featured Paul dancing in an art gallery amidst sixteen females all wearing matching black business suits and red wigs. The choreography was patterned after Paul's own dance moves.

Paul McCartney – vocals, electric guitar, harpsichord, keyboards, bass, drums, tambourine

186. DANCE TONIGHT
Paul McCartney

Written by Paul McCartney
Recorded January 2007
Released June 5, 2007
Album: MEMORY ALMOST FULL

A Christmas present Paul bought for himself led to the opening cut on *Memory Almost Full*. On his way to a meeting, he stopped to visit his favorite guitar shop in London. Asking the clerk if they had any new "lefties," he was shown a left-handed mandolin they had gotten in. Tuned like a violin rather than a guitar, Paul wouldn't know how to play it, but knew he'd be inspired and likened it to the wonder of getting his first guitar.

Enjoying the challenge of figuring out chords, he was in his kitchen strumming away, stomping his feet, and singing "Everybody gonna dance tonight!" when his three-year-old daughter Beatrice ran in and started dancing. From there, Paul says the song wrote itself and he kept the mandolin as its signature instrument.

In the studio, Paul played all the instruments himself. To give the song a vintage treatment, he employed old-school effects including stomping on a piece of wood to provide the song's insistent beat. For additional percussion, the studio's air conditioning grille was removed so Paul could play it like a washboard.

"Dance Tonight" was the last song recorded for *Memory Almost Full*, an album that got its name from the recurring message on Paul's cellphone.

Fellow vegetarian Natalie Portman (*Black Swan*) stars as a dancing ghost in the promo video directed by Michel Gondry (*Eternal Sunshine of the Spotless Mind*). She was suggested for the video by Paul's daughter Stella, from whom Portman bought designer shoes. Portman would also be featured in the video for Paul's "My Valentine" in 2012.

Paul McCartney – vocals, mandolin, lead guitar, bass, keyboard, autoharp, drums, percussion

187. NOD YOUR HEAD
Paul McCartney

Written by Paul McCartney
Recorded March 2006
Released August 28, 2007
Album: MEMORY ALMOST FULL

Visiting George Harrison a few weeks before his death in 2001, Paul had marveled that his former bandmate, in pain and facing the inevitable, managed to remain upbeat. They shared jokes and reminisced about their early days together. After losing three of his closest companions in addition to both of his parents, Paul knew the value of dealing with death rather than shying away from it.

Memory Almost Full includes a medley in which Paul looks back at his personal history, starting with his school days and continuing into his life of fame. The final song, "The End of the End", is his touching final request: when he dies, he wants jokes to be told, songs to be sung, and stories of old to be rolled out like carpets for children to play on and lovers to lay on. There's no reason to cry, he sings, because the end of the end is "the start of a journey to a much better place."

Appropriately, it was to be the last song on *Memory Almost Full,* but Paul and producer David Kahne decided it wasn't prudent to leave listeners hanging with a tearjerker. So Paul came up with a new closer, the rambunctious "Nod Your Head", to lift spirits back up.

At just under two minutes, the short but effective mood changer was also released as a free iTunes single. In the grunge rocker, Paul gives detailed instructions on how to vigorously nod your head in agreement if "you like the life you're living."

This affirmative form of headbanging is demonstrated in the music video, in which Paul, Ringo and Barbara are joined by fashion models, a concert audience, and a pair of Weimaraners obediently performing the imagined dance craze.

Paul McCartney – vocals, piano, keyboards, synthesizer, bass,
    electric guitar, drums

188. LIVERPOOL 8
Ringo Starr

Written by Richard Starkey and Dave Stewart
Recorded 2007
Released December 4, 2007
Album: LIVERPOOL 8

Reuniting with Capitol Records after a long separation, Ringo's next album, *Liverpool 8,* featured a title track he co-wrote with former Eurythmic Dave Stewart. Largely about the Fab Four, "Liverpool 8" takes its name from the postal code where Ringo was born.

The autobiographical ode traces his career from a teenage gig as a ferry barman to drumming for Rory Storm to attaining fame with the Beatles. He sings of leaving his birthplace on Madryn Street and his childhood home in Admiral Grove because destiny was calling. Ringo performed the song in Liverpool in front of 50,000 at the city's January celebration as the 2008 European Capital of Culture.

A week later, Ringo was asked by British interviewer Jonathan Ross if he missed Liverpool. "Uh, no," he answered. Jovially but without apology, his follow-up remarks left no doubt that he hadn't left his heart in Liverpool. This didn't sit well with Liverpudlians, who felt betrayed to the point of lopping off his head from a life-sized topiary of the Beatles. John, Paul and George were left unharmed.

In the minds of many, the man who had just sung "Liverpool, I left you but I never let you down" disagreed. *Liverpool 8* debuted at a humiliating #94 on the Billboard album charts, and sales were equally disappointing.

Later that year, Ringo announced that he would no longer be signing autographs.

Ringo Starr – vocals, drums, percussion
Dave Stewart – acoustic guitar, electric guitar
Sean Hurley – bass
Gary Burr, Steve Dudas, Brent Carpenter, Mark Hudson, Bruce
   Sugar, Keith Allison – backing vocals, handclaps

189. SING THE CHANGES
The Fireman (Paul McCartney and Youth)

Written by Paul McCartney
Recorded December 2007
Released December 16, 2008
Album: ELECTRIC ARGUMENTS

At the end of 2007, Paul reunited with Youth for a third collaboration of experimental music. This time around, rather than repurposing existing recordings, Paul wrote entirely new compositions. The duo recorded one song a day over the course of thirteen days, spread out over several months. The sessions took place at Paul's home studio, The Mill.

Performing all of the instrumentation himself, Paul approached each song with no idea of where it would go, much less what the melody or lyrics would be about. The impromptu challenge, he felt, brought a certain electricity to the project. Only once the music track was down did he record vocals, coming up with largely improvised lyrics.

"Sing the Changes" is a stream-of-consciousness invocation to experience and celebrate life: to feel the quiet, feel the thunder, feel childlike wonder, and to sing praises as you're sleeping. Paul found it fascinating to explore unrelated word combinations. The album title, *Electric Arguments*, was taken from a poem by Allen Ginsberg.

Awash in reverb, "Sing the Changes" has an anthem-like quality with a continuously repeating melody of four measures. For an experimental song, it was commercial enough that Paul would include it in concerts.

This time around, The Fireman recognized the futility of attempting anonymity. Aided by a promotional video in which Paul appeared prominently, Paul and Youth's third album project sold much better than their previous outings and was acclaimed by critics as one of the best albums of 2008.

Paul McCartney – vocals, acoustic guitar, electric guitar, mandolin, keyboards, bass, drums, tambourine

190. MEAT FREE MONDAY
Paul McCartney

Written by Paul McCartney
Recorded 2009
Released June 9, 2009
Digital download

When Paul was young, one of his favorite meals was lamb chops. He regarded vegetarians as wimps. But a Sunday lunch in 1975 changed his point of view. Looking out his farm window at little lambs frolicking, the leg of lamb he was eating lost all its appeal. From that point on, he and Linda famously became vegetarians.

"One day a week can make a world of difference," says the website meatfreemondays.com, a nonprofit campaign created in 2009 by Paul and his daughters Mary and Stella. The idea behind Meat Free Mondays is to encourage people to forgo meat products one day a week and, in so doing, realize how easy it could be to become a full-time vegetarian.

From the McCartneys' perspective, a plant-based diet is not only kinder to animals, it reduces greenhouse gases, conserves natural resources, and alleviates world hunger. To eliminate livestock production and industrial fishing, they assert, would be an environmental boon of infinite proportions.

A series of videos promoting the campaign were created, with Paul hosting several of them. To mark the launch of Meat Free Mondays, he debuted a simple jingle on video and encouraged viewers to send in their recipes. He soon recorded a more fully developed theme song with lyrics that flesh out the evils of eating meat. The infectious chorus fades at the end alongside a chugging "Strawberry Fields Forever" drumbeat. The song was offered as a free download.

Along with fellow celebrities including Sheryl Crow and Woody Harrelson, the McCartneys' meat-free mission is endorsed by leading chefs who create vegetarian recipes for the official website.

Paul McCartney – vocals, piano, electric guitar, bass, drums

191. WALK WITH YOU
Ringo Starr

Written by Richard Starkey and Van Dyke Parks
Recorded February 2009
Released December 22, 2009
Album: Y NOT

Y Not, Ringo's 16th studio album, was the first on which he took the helm as producer. At his Los Angeles home studio, he experimented with Pro Tools recording software and synthesizers he had on hand. Having fun and building tracks until something substantial developed, he would then call musician friends and invite them to finish writing the songs.

One such call was to Van Dyke Parks, a collaborator of note who had served as lyricist for no less than Brian Wilson. Ringo told Parks he wanted to write a "gospelly" song. Responding that he doesn't write "God songs," Parks dismissed Ringo's worshipful inclination and persuaded him to make "Walk with You" a tribute to the power of friendship instead.

Paul, in town for the Grammy Awards, visited Ringo's studio to record a bass track for another *Y Not* song, "Peace Dream". While there, Ringo played him some of the other album tracks. "Walk with You" wasn't intended to be a duet, but when Paul heard it, he had an idea for a harmony that comes in slightly behind Ringo's lead vocal. The result became the song's catchy calling card, a nostalgic treat for Beatles fans as the two old friends unite in their first-ever duet.

The single "Walk with You" marked Paul's first release after a lengthy and particularly acrimonious divorce from Heather Mills. The couple parted in March 2008.

Ringo Starr – vocals, drums, percussion
Paul McCartney – vocals, bass
Steve Dudas – guitar
Ann Marie Calhoun – violin
Bruce Sugar – keyboards

192. (I WANT TO) COME HOME
Paul McCartney

Written by Paul McCartney
Recorded June 2009
Released March 1, 2010
Album: CD single

For the 2009 film *Everybody's Fine,* Paul was asked by director Kirk Jones to write a song to accompany a poignant scene in the Robert De Niro drama. Jones showed Paul a rough cut of the movie with Aretha Franklin's version of "Let It Be" temporarily filling the space Paul's song would occupy. Paul found it easy to identify with the main character, a widower with older children who tries to reconnect with all of them at Christmas.

His wistful ballad speaks of shooting for the stars for too long and wanting to come home where sweet memories lie waiting. Although Paul wrote the song from the perspective of the widower, it occurred to him afterwards that it could also represent the thoughts of the adult children.

Paul recorded a cassette demo and sent it to Jones for suggestions, upon which the director requested an instrumental prelude instead of a cold start. After adding a five-bar piano intro, Paul worked with the film's soundtrack composer Dario Marianelli to create orchestration. Paul otherwise plays all of the instruments.

Winning a Critic's Choice award, "(I Want to) Come Home" was released as a CD single but did not appear on the soundtrack album.

These days, Paul was coming home to Nancy Shevell, an American businesswomen and heiress in a transportation conglomerate. They had known each other socially for many years, but after recent divorces for both of them, Nancy's cousin Barbara Walters began an earnest campaign to make them a couple. Her matchmaking advice to Nancy: "Look at Heather Mills, and do exactly the opposite."

Paul McCartney – vocals, acoustic guitar, electric guitar, piano, bass, drums, tambourine

193. MY VALENTINE
Paul McCartney

Written by Paul McCartney
Recorded Spring 2011
Released December 20, 2011
Album: KISSES ON THE BOTTOM

What would have been John Lennon's 71st birthday was also Paul and Nancy Shevell's wedding day on October 9, 2011. Paul's eight-year-old daughter Beatrice served as flower girl at the same Marylebone town hall where Paul and Linda were wed in 1969. At the reception, Sir Paul revealed "My Valentine", which he had written for now-Lady Nancy earlier that year.

The couple had been on a February vacation in Morocco when rain threatened to dampen their spirits. Paul expressed regret about the weather, but Nancy responded that it didn't matter and they could still have a good time. On Valentine's Day, sitting at the hotel piano, Paul found chords for his opening lyric: "What if it rained? We didn't care. She said that someday soon the sun was gonna shine."

Recalling the mood of the 1937 standard "My Funny Valentine", the melancholy but thoroughly romantic tune was recorded live with Diana Krall on piano and a guitar solo added later by Eric Clapton. While overdubbing the latter at Abbey Road, Paul realized that the last time they had been in that studio together was forty years earlier, when Clapton did the solo on "While My Guitar Gently Weeps". Johnny Depp performed a similar guitar solo on the music video, joined by Natalie Portman conveying the lyrics in sign language.

Paul McCartney – vocals
Diana Krall – piano
Eric Clapton – lead guitar
John Pizzarelli – guitar
Robert Hurst – bass
Karriem Riggins – drums
London Symphony Orchestra – strings

194. ONLY OUR HEARTS
Paul McCartney

Written by Paul McCartney
Recorded March 2010
Released February 6, 2012
Album: KISSES ON THE BOTTOM

The classic tunes of Harold Arlen and Cole Porter were an influence on Paul long before Buddy Holly and Chuck Berry. Now in his sixties, Paul felt it was an appropriate time to pay homage to the music that started it all with an album of standards and a couple of his newer compositions written in the same style.

Though the album was originally to be called *My Valentine* after its featured single, Paul was concerned that it might be regarded as a holiday release and have a short shelf life. He suggested the title *Kisses on the Bottom*, to which all of his collaborators gave a resounding "No!" After Paul clarified its vague reference to lipstick prints on the bottom of a love letter, the playful double entendre made the grade and gave the album the informal first impression he was going for.

In "Only Our Hearts", Paul longs for his lover to be nearer. While he and Nancy Shevell were dating, she was still based in New York and he was usually in London. Their long-distance romance often saw him serenading her by phone with his latest song.

Recorded in L.A. with an ensemble totally different from the rest of the songs on *Kisses on the Bottom*, this second single features a harmonica solo by Stevie Wonder. It was his first time recording with Paul since 1982's "Ebony and Ivory". After listening to "Only Our Hearts" in the studio, Wonder nailed his solo in 20 minutes.

Paul McCartney – vocals
Stevie Wonder – harmonica
John Chiodini – guitar
Tamir Hendelman – piano
Chuck Berghoffer – bass
Vinnie Colauita – drums

195. THE CHRISTMAS SONG (CHESTNUTS ROASTING ON AN OPEN FIRE)
Paul McCartney

Written by Mel Tormé and Robert Wells
Recorded Spring 2011
Released October 30, 2012
Album: HOLIDAYS RULE (various artists)

Paul had wanted to do an album of standards since the Beatles days, but with former rockers like Rod Stewart and Linda Rondstadt already crooning the Great American Songbook, he didn't want to look like he was jumping on the bandwagon. So his 2011 sessions with Diana Krall focused on classics that were less predictable.

Even so, he couldn't resist recording the holiday chestnut "The Christmas Song", made famous by Nat King Cole and covered thousands of times. To include a yuletide tune on the album would have seemed an odd addition, so it was instead given to Hear Music for their 2011 indie artist collection *Holidays Rule*.

The song was written by Bob Wells and Mel Tormé on a particularly hot summer day in 1945. Simply wanting to beat the heat, Wells tried to stay cool by "thinking cool." He wrote down the phrases "Chestnuts roasting," "Jack Frost nipping," "yuletide carols" and "folks dressed up like Eskimos" in his notebook. When collaborator Tormé spotted the wordings, he felt a song coming on, and a Christmas classic was written by the Jewish songwriters in forty minutes.

Paul's version was released as both red and green 7" vinyl singles. In keeping with his vegetarian virtues, he changed the line "a turkey and some mistletoe" to "some holly and some mistletoe."

Paul McCartney – vocals
Diana Krall – piano
Eric Clapton – lead guitar
John Pizzarelli – guitar
Robert Hurst – bass
Karriem Riggins – drums

196. NEW
Paul McCartney

Written by Paul McCartney
Recorded January 2012
Released September 2, 2013
Album: NEW

After balladeering on *Kisses on the Bottom*, Paul was ready to rock again and—seeking the pulse of what was popular—allied with hot young producers for his next album project, simply titled *New*.

Producer Mark Ronson (Christina Aguilera, Amy Winehouse) started out as a club DJ and continued to be highly sought-after in that capacity for high-profile galas and private parties. Paul hired him for a couple of his own events, including his wedding to Nancy Shevell, and enlisted him as one of the four producers on his new album.

In the studio, Paul applauded producer Ronson for his energy, expertise and enthusiasm, qualities present on the title track and first single from *New*. Written late at night at Paul's London home on his father's old piano, "New" features a pounding Penny Lane-like rhythm and lyrics pertaining to the optimism of new love.

Although Paul's touring band had continued to perform with him throughout the previous decade, his new album marked the first time they recorded together since 2001's *Driving Rain*. On his last three albums, he had performed all of the instruments himself or sang to the accompaniment of guest musicians.

> Paul McCartney – vocals, piano, harpsichord, electric piano, bass, Mellotron, bouzouki, congas, maracas
> Rusty Anderson – guitar, bouzouki, backing vocals
> Brian Ray – guitar, backing vocals
> Abe Laboriel, Jr. – drums, backing vocals
> Paul "Wix" Wickens – backing vocals
> Steve Sidwell – trumpet
> Jamie Talbot – tenor saxophone
> Dave Bishop – baritone saxophone

197. QUEENIE EYE
Paul McCartney

Written by Paul McCartney and Paul Epworth
Recorded January 2012
Released October 24, 2013
Album: NEW

"Queenie Eye", the second single from *New*, was one of several songs produced by Paul Epworth, who had produced songs by Adele and Florence + the Machine. Epworth's studio approach was to jam with Paul until they came up with a riff worth turning into a song. Paul said "Queenie Eye" started out very raw but came to life with the addition of drums and synthesizers.

As a youngster, one of the street games Paul played was known as "Queenie Eye". In it, a player throws a ball over his shoulder, turns, and has to guess who caught the ball as they tease, "Queenie Eye, Queenie Eye, who's got the ball? I haven't got it, it isn't in my pocket, O-U-T spells OUT." Paul liked the cadence of that chant and used it as the chorus of "Queenie Eye". (Beatles fan club members will recall that Ringo had first immortalized the phrase "O-U-T spells OUT" on 1967's "Christmas Time Is Here Again".)

Relating the playground game to the game of life, Paul sings of rules he had to learn on his own and wicked witches who fan the flame and hunt for fame. Mentioned is the moral of the story: to never pick a battle you know you'll lose.

"Queenie Eye" was originally to be the opening song on the album but was replaced by "Save Us." A star-studded video directed by Simon Aboud—the husband of Paul's daughter Mary—was filmed at the famous Abbey Road Studio 2. Among those surrounding Paul and his piano are Johnny Depp, Meryl Streep, Tracy Ullman, Jude Law, Kate Moss, Jeremy Irons, Chris Pine, James Corden and Sean Penn.

Paul McCartney – vocals, guitar, steel guitar, piano, synthesizer,
    Mellotron, bass, tambourine
Paul Epworth – drums

198. EVERYBODY OUT THERE
Paul McCartney

Written by Paul McCartney
Recorded February 2013
Released 2013
Album: NEW

Giles Martin, son of producer George Martin, has known Paul all his life. Now that he had become a popular producer in his own right (Kate Bush, Elton John, Jeff Beck), the younger Martin was approached by Paul to be one of the producers of his new album. Martin was reticent because he knew Paul so well and thought it might be detrimental to their good relationship. But "you don't say no to Paul," he said.

Martin was pleasantly surprised to discover that Paul preferred having someone tell him what to do in the studio, versus having to both perform and produce himself. Martin says Paul was the artist who made him feel valued for his own talents rather than for being the son of the legendary fifth Beatle.

Among the first songs Martin produced for *New* was the single "Everybody Out There". Paul wrote the "make a difference" song with concert crowds in mind, to give them a chant to sing along with.

Paul McCartney – vocals, guitar, piano, keyboards, Mellotron, bass
Rusty Anderson – guitar
Brian Ray – guitar
Toby Pitman - keyboards
Abe Laboriel, Jr. – drums
Giles Martin – foot stomp
McCartney family – backing vocals
Cathy Thompson, Patrick Kiernan, Nina Foster, Laura Melhuish – violin
Peter Lale, Rachel Robson – viola
Caroline Dale, Katherine Jenkinson, Chris Worsey – cello
Steve McManus, Richard Pryce – double bass
Eliza Marshall, Anna Noakes – alto flute

199. SAVE US
Paul McCartney

Written by Paul McCartney and Paul Epworth
Recorded January 2012
Released March 31, 2014
Album: NEW

The first sessions for *New* took place at producer Paul Epworth's London studio. In anticipation of recording the album, Paul had written roughly twenty songs. Surprised to discover that Epworth's modus operandi was to create magic spontaneously in the studio, Paul saved his existing song ideas for the other producers he would be working with on the album.

The fourth single from *New* sprung forth from Paul and Epworth's very first jam session. For their initial effort, Epworth told Paul he was inclined to do something "punky." With Paul on bass and Epworth on drums, they arrived at a catchy riff within a half hour. After working out chords on the piano, they built up the track with Paul overdubbing bass and fuzz-heavy guitars.

When it came time for vocals, Epworth asked Paul to step up to the mic. Paul protested that there were no lyrics yet, but Epworth encouraged him to improvise and not overthink it. The aggressive character of the music inspired adlibbed in-your-face lyrics that Paul says he pulled out of nowhere and refined over the course of a few takes. Unconvinced of their merit, he gave a disclaimer to the engineers that the song might be rubbish. However, the energetic "Save Us" ended up being chosen as the strong opening track on *New*.

Like much of the semi-autobiographical material on the album, "Save Us"—praising the saving power of love—gained much of its inspiration from his marriage to Nancy Shevell. Both joy and sadness are explored throughout *New*, and Paul credited his new wife for bringing him back into a more fulfilling period in his life.

Paul McCartney – vocals, electric guitars, bass, piano
Paul Epworth – drums

200. APPRECIATE
Paul McCartney

Written by Paul McCartney
Recorded April 2013
Released May 16, 2014
Album: NEW

Serving as executive producer on *New* was Giles Martin, who by now had added his own name to the Fab Four pantheon, having remastered their music for Cirque du Soleil's Beatles-themed show *Love*, Martin Scorsese's Harrison documentary *Living in the Material World*, and *The Beatles Rock Band* video game. "Appreciate" was one of five songs produced for *New* by Martin.

Experimenting with tape loops by layering them into a sound collage, neither Paul nor Martin were certain that it was song material until Paul incorporated a chorus he had previously written.

"Appreciate" showcases Paul's falsetto vocal against an ethereal backdrop which occasionally breaks into a raucous bridge of distorted guitars and rapid-fire lyrics about reciprocating love. Paul called it a "weird little track" but a "great one to make." Contributing to the unique instrumentation was a Greek bouzouki and a ciguitar, a guitar made from a cigar box.

The unconventional feel of the song lent itself well to the futuristic promo video, which had its origins in an image Paul woke up with one morning of standing next to a large robot. He thought it could make a good album cover but would have been too reminiscent of the android on Ringo's *Goodnight Vienna*. Instead, the robot encounters Paul in the video's "Museum of Man", where Paul comes to life and tries to convey humanity to the metal man. The robot ("Newman") was designed and performed by the puppeteers of the hit stage show *War Horse*.

.

Paul McCartney – vocals, guitar, ciguitar, keyboards, drums
Rusty Anderson – guitar, bouzouki, backing vocals
Brian Ray – guitar, backing vocals
Abe Laboriel, Jr. – drums, backing vocals

201. EARLY DAYS
Paul McCartney

Written by Paul McCartney
Recorded March 2013
Released July 7, 2014
Album: NEW

Another producer Paul worked with on his new album was Ethan Johns, the son of veteran engineer Glyn Johns (The Rolling Stones, Eric Clapton, The Beatles). It was Johns' work with Kings of Leon that led Paul to approach him to co-produce *New*.

The single "Early Days" had an agenda to convey, namely that no one knows the whole truth about The Beatles except The Beatles. While on vacation, Paul encountered a young American girl on the beach who told him about the Beatles Appreciation class she had taken at school. After he shared a funny inside story he thought she might enjoy, she replied, "No, that's not what happened. We covered that in my class." Incidents like that were too common.

On the day he wrote the song, Paul had been reminiscing about his teenage years visiting record shops with John. The joy of listening to the latest American rock and roll and writing songs together is something no one can ever take away from him, the song says.

"Early Days" features rustic instrumentation befitting its '50s theme, including Paul's double bass once owned by Bill Black. Paul wasn't happy with his vocal, often creaky and weathered, but producer Johns convinced him that it gave the song authenticity.

The music video for "Early Days" was the third in which Johnny Depp made a cameo. Paul quipped that Depp had become his Alfred Hitchcock.

Paul McCartney – vocals, guitar, bass, harmonium, knee slaps
Ethan Johns – drums, percussion
Brian Ray – dulcimer
Rusty Anderson – slide guitar
Abe Laboriel, Jr. – backing vocals

202. HOPE FOR THE FUTURE
Paul McCartney

Written by Paul McCartney
Recorded September 20, 2012–March 2013
Released December 8, 2014
Album: DESTINY (video game)

Bungie, the studio behind the popular video game *Halo*, approached Paul in 2011 to see if he'd be interested in doing music for their next project, *Destiny*. Always interested in expanding his audience base, Paul co-wrote soundtrack music for the 2014 online multiplayer game. "Hope for the Future" plays over the end credits.

In the game, the player is entrusted with guarding the last remaining city on Earth. Inspired by the idea of being the world's only hope, Paul set about writing this futuristic song. Reminding himself that it wasn't just a song for a game but also needed to stand alone, he avoided mentions of aliens or any specific game play.

The basic track was recorded with his band at Paul's studio in Sussex. An orchestra was overdubbed later at Abbey Road along with Libera, a famed boys choir.

With a vast cosmic soundscape worthy of Epcot, "Hope for the Future" was available as a digital download and a 12-inch vinyl single with multiple mixes. As for the game itself, worldwide sales of *Destiny* reached $325 million worldwide in its first week.

Paul himself only plays video games when he sees his grandchildren playing them. He says he tries "for two seconds, gets killed, and then hands the controls back to the grandkids."

Paul McCartney – vocals, guitar, piano
Rusty Anderson – lead guitar
Paul "Wix" Wickens – keyboards
Brian Ray – bass
Abe Laboriel, Jr – drums
Toby Pitman – keyboard programming
Caroline Dale – cello
Libera – boys choir

203. POSTCARDS FROM PARADISE
Ringo Starr

Written by Richard Starkey and Todd Rundgren
Recorded 2014
Released March 3, 2015
Album: POSTCARDS FROM PARADISE

Todd Rundgren ("Hello, It's Me", "I Saw the Light") first played with Ringo in 1979 as part of a supergroup during a Jerry Lewis Muscular Dystrophy telethon. He remembers that they had to back up fiddle player Doug Kershaw, who wouldn't stop playing "Jambalaya". So they kept speeding up the tempo until he couldn't keep up anymore.

In the late '90s, Rundgren began participating in Ringo's All-Starr Band for the occasional tour. Rundgren co-wrote the title track and the single for Ringo's 18th solo album *Postcards from Paradise*.

A mixed bag of pop, rock and reggae, the entire album was produced by Ringo and recorded at his home studio. Each of the songs began as a drum track, after which Ringo would invite a songwriting partner to collaborate with him on the music and lyrics. Ringo and Rundgren developed "Postcards from Paradise" with a dreamy "Within You Without You" melody and lyrics that reference over two dozen Beatle and Ringo songs from "Love Me Do" to "Back Off Boogaloo". Ringo's now-brother-in-law Joe Walsh provided a Harrisonesque guitar solo to complete the pastiche.

"Postcards from Paradise" was released as a single a few weeks before Ringo was given the Award for Musical Excellence by the Rock and Roll Hall of Fame in Cleveland, Ohio. Paul McCartney was there to present the award on April 18, 2015. Upon this induction, all four Beatles were now in the Rock and Roll Hall of Fame as individuals. They had been inducted as a group in 1988.

Ringo Starr – vocals, drums, keyboards
Todd Rundgren – backing vocals
Joe Walsh – electric guitar
Bruce Sugar – piano, synthesizer

204. GIVE MORE LOVE
Ringo Starr

Written by Richard Starkey and Gary Nicholson
Recorded 2017
Released July 17, 2017
Album: GIVE MORE LOVE

In 2016, Ringo intended to go to Nashville and create a country album. Instead, he went on tour in America and Asia before returning to the studio. While some of the songs on 2017's "Give More Love" have a twang to them, they are mostly rock oriented and were recorded at Roccabella West, Ringo's home studio in L.A.

The first single—its title track—was released on Ringo's 77th birthday on July 7, 2017. Ringo wrote "Give More Love" with Nashville composer Gary Nicholson, whose songs have been recorded over 500 times by both country and rock artists from Garth Brooks to Stevie Nicks.

Like most of Ringo's hits, the message of "Give More Love" falls into the "All You Need Is Love" category. He sings that the world can be a hard place with broken hearts and angry words, but peace and love are the answer.

Just prior to the recording session, Ringo had received the gift of a Hang, a type of steel drum played by hand rather than with a mallet. The melodic instrument is best heard during the intro and the choruses.

Ringo ran a contest inviting fans to send in photos and videos that represented what giving more love meant to them. The images Ringo liked best appeared in his "Give More Love" music video as if they were in a Rolodex flip file.

Ringo Starr – vocals, drums, percussion
Steve Dudas – guitar
Jim Cox – piano
Matt Bissonette – bass
Gregg Bissonette – Hang percussion
Amy Keys, Richard Page, Timothy B. Schmidt – backing vocals

205. WE'RE ON THE ROAD AGAIN
Ringo Starr

Written by Richard Starkey and Steve Lukather
Recorded 2017
Released July 28, 2017
Album: GIVE MORE LOVE

Steve Lukather of Toto, who had just been on the road with Ringo, created the hyperactive guitar lick that characterizes the second single from *Give More Love*. A true road song, "We're on the Road Again" opens the album.

Co-written with Lukather (or Luke, as Ringo calls him), the song originated when the two were just "hanging out" and happened upon a rhythm pattern that inspired them to lay down a track. The lively tune developed into a celebration of life on the concert circuit, one of sharing stories on tour buses and planes while counting the hours till they can be back on stage playing the rock and roll they love.

They had initial concerns that the title and theme would be too similar to Willie Nelson's 1980 country hit "On the Road Again", but since their song was a rocker—and because they added "We're" to the title—they opted to let it be.

Paul was in Los Angeles recording his own upcoming album, so Ringo asked if he'd be willing to play on his. Paul came in on a Sunday, his day off, and participated in two songs, this and "Show Me the Way". For "We're on the Road Again" he contributed an intricate bass line as well as a scream. Ringo hadn't asked Paul to scream; it was spontaneous and genuine. Ringo remarked that real rock and roll and screams simply go together.

Ringo Starr – vocals, drums, percussion
Paul McCartney – bass, backing vocals
Steve Lukather – guitar, keyboards, backing vocals
Jim Cox – keyboards
Joe Walsh, Edgar Winter, Gary Burr, Georgia Middleman – backing
   vocals

206. SO WRONG FOR SO LONG
Ringo Starr

Written by Richard Starkey and Dave Stewart
Recorded 2017
Released August 18, 2017
Album: GIVE MORE LOVE

Ringo's 19th studio album featured ten new songs plus new versions of four of his previous songs, including 1968's "Don't Pass Me By", one of Ringo's first attempts at writing a country song. In 2016, when he thought his album would be recorded in Nashville, he and Dave Stewart decided to write some country songs at Ringo's house. The first one they collaborated on, "So Wrong for So Long", became the album's third single.

Many Beatle fans know it was Ringo who came up with the title for "A Hard Day's Night". As he tells it, it was at the end of a long working day when he said, "It's been a hard day—" and, suddenly realizing how late it had gotten, added, "night." Paul and John said Ringo was notorious for similar slips and quips, many of which wound up in song.

Whether writing alone or with a collaborator, Ringo says his songs usually start with a single idea, so he keeps a list of phrases to use as starting points. In the case of "So Wrong for So Long", someone else spoke those words to Ringo back in 2008, and he felt it would make an ideal country song title one day.

The verses describe a romance that sounds like a match made in Heaven with a couple as perfect as "Johnny Cash and June," but in the choruses he says that he was mistaken. Only in the last verse does he reveal why.

Ringo Starr – vocals, drums, percussion
Dave Stewart – guitar
Greg Leisz – pedal steel guitar
Jim Cox – keyboards
Nathan East – upright bass
Gary Burr, Georgia Middleman – backing vocals

207. STANDING STILL
Ringo Starr

Written by Richard Starkey and Gary Burr
Recorded 2017
Released September 8, 2017
Album: GIVE MORE LOVE

From their Fab Four days forward, each of the Beatles have used music to promote a better world. John's radical approach, meant to shock people into submission, had its counterpart in George's more spiritual quest for enlightenment. Whenever Paul does musical commentary, it tends to be rooted in saving the planet. Ringo, meanwhile, has made "peace and love" his ongoing mantra, and more than any ex-Beatle has gained the reputation for feel-good songs with a simple message.

Ringo says he puts out friendly, positive songs because he feels blessed to have good friends who happen to be excellent musicians with whom he can have fun doing what he loves most. His open-door policy means anyone who comes by to say hi is likely to end up writing a song with him, playing an instrument on his next album, or doing a guest appearance in his All-Star Band.

"Standing Still", the fourth single from *Give More Love*, is Ringo's advice not to let life pass one by. Co-writer Gary Burr and his wife Georgia Middleman sing backup, and a dobro played by award-winning session musician Greg Leisz adds a bluesy Southern feel.

Ringo still intends to record some country music. One of the first pop stars to have recorded in Nashville back in 1970, Ringo remarked that these days Nashville has been coming to him.

Ringo Starr – vocals, percussion, claps
Greg Leisz – dobro
Steve Dudas – guitar
Gary Burr – acoustic guitar, backing vocals
Nathan East – upright bass
Bruce Sugar – drum programming
Georgia Middleman – backing vocals

208. I DON'T KNOW
Paul McCartney

Written by Paul McCartney
Recorded 2017
Released June 20, 2018
Album: EGYPT STATION

In 2016, Paul signed a historic worldwide deal with Capitol Records—the Beatles' first American record company—encompassing his entire immense catalog of recordings starting with his 1970 solo album *McCartney*. He mentioned with full-circle satisfaction that the first record he ever bought had been a Capitol record, Gene Vincent's "Be-Bop-a-Lula".

Paul's new album with his reunited label was *Egypt Station*, produced by Greg Kurstin (Beck, Adele, Foo Fighters). Paul had previously worked with Kurstin on a yet-to-be-released animation project with Lady Gaga. The two worked on *Egypt Station* off and on over the course of two years, alternating between touring and other commitments.

The first single from *Egypt Station* was the plaintive piano ballad "I Don't Know". Paul wrote it following a personal episode in his life in which he doubted himself. He explained that bad times can be good times to write because it comes from the soul, and that admitting "I don't know what to do" is "owning up." Getting it all out in a song was better than going to a psychiatrist, he said, adding that John Lennon would have liked this one.

Kurstin noted that the unique chord changes of "I Don't Know" sound original and yet oddly familiar courtesy of a "nursery-rhyme melody" that pulls it all together. Paul plays most of the instruments, with support from Kurstin and guest percussionist Rob Millett, who plays cimbalom, a bright, ringing instrument in the dulcimer family.

Paul McCartney – vocals, piano, keyboards, acoustic guitar, bass,
    drums, percussion
Greg Kurstin – keyboards, electric guitar, Mellotron
Rob Millett – cimbalom

209. COME ON TO ME
Paul McCartney

Written by Paul McCartney
Recorded 2017
Released June 20, 2018
Album: EGYPT STATION

Along with "I Don't Know", "Come On to Me" made up the double-sided single to promote Paul's upcoming album *Egypt Station*.

Paul called the fictional "Come On to Me" a pick-up song for the older generation, although its inspiration came from the memory of parties he'd attended in his twenties, where he'd spot a beautiful girl who may or may not be flirting, and question the rules of engagement.

The upbeat song with a stomping beat imagines Paul catching someone's eye at a party and pondering the chemistry that might ensue. Interpreting the stranger's smile as an invitation to more than casual conversation, he asks outright whether she came on to him and, if so, he'll gladly return the favor.

The verses and choruses share essentially the same chords and melody until an instrumental break changes things up at 1:53 with a simulated sitar followed by the Muscle Shoals Rhythm Section.

Paul debuted "Come On to Me" during a surprise live performance at a Liverpool eatery in conjunction with the taping of a special episode of James Corden's "Carpool Karaoke".

Paul McCartney – vocals, electric and acoustic guitars, keyboards, percussion, harmonica
Paul "Wix" Wickens – keyboards
Rusty Anderson – electric guitar
Brian Ray – electric guitar, bass
Abe Laboriel, Jr. – drums
Greg Phillinganes – piano
Tim Loo – cello
Greg Kurstin – electric guitar, percussion
Muscle Shoals Rhythm Section – horns

210. FUH YOU
Paul McCartney

Written by Paul McCartney and Ryan Tedder
Recorded 2017
Released August 15, 2018
Album: EGYPT STATION

Three weeks prior to the release of *Egypt Station*, Paul released a third single, the oddly titled (and spelled) "Fuh You".

A scheduling conflict saw producer Greg Kurstin unavailable during one of Paul's free weeks to record, so he brought in Ryan Tedder of the band OneRepublic ("Counting Stars", "Apologize"), who had written and produced for U2, Jennifer Lopez, the Jonas Brothers, and many others. Paul and Tedder co-wrote "Fuh You" and two other songs later released as singles.

Paul had a number of songs ready to record, but he and Tedder decided to use the spontaneous songwriting approach that had worked on Paul's most recent albums. Starting from scratch, they found a beat they liked, built it up, and then dabbled with words.

In the song, Paul encourages his lady to talk about herself candidly and let him get to know her. Allowing her to express her real self is a gift, and he just wants it "fuh" her. Admitting that there is mischief afoot, Paul called it "sort of a love song, but a raunchy love song." To restore some decorum, a string quintet was brought in, but radio stations still weren't about to play "Fuh You" and it didn't chart.

Its black and white promo video stars a teenage boy (actor Harry Wyatt) lip-syncing as he walks home jubilantly after kissing a girl.

Paul McCartney – vocals, piano, electric piano, harpsichord
Ryan Tedder – backing vocals
David Angell – violin
Alicia Enstrom – violin
Betsy Lamb – viola
Paul Nelson – cello
Jack Jezzro – double bass

211. BACK IN BRAZIL
Paul McCartney

Written by Paul McCartney
Recorded October 2017
Released September 16, 2018
Album: EGYPT STATION

Paul set a world's record for largest concert audience by a solo artist in 1990 when 184,000 fans flooded Rio de Janeiro during his world tour. October 2017 saw Paul back in Brazil to do shows in four cities. On one of his days off in São Paulo, he found himself with some alone time. After breakfast and a visit to the gym, he killed time by playing the Wurlitzer electric piano in his hotel suite. Arriving at a chord sequence with a catchy rhythm best described as Latin lounge, he wrote "Back in Brazil".

The lyrics tell an imaginary story of a Brazilian girl searching for something better. She meets a man who meets her criteria, and all seems right until his work gets in the way of their relationship.

A portion of the lyrics had yet to be written, so Paul blocked it out with "hechibam," a made-up word that sounded Brazilian and would do the trick until he found a suitable replacement. Later, while getting a massage from a therapist who happened to be Japanese, the word "ichiban" came up in conversation. Even though the word wasn't Portuguese, Paul liked its similarity to "hechibam", especially when he learned that it meant "the best." Before leaving Brazil, Paul recorded the masseuse's friends shouting "Ichiban!" to use on the track.

The instrumental solo features Venezuelan flautist Pedro Eustache playing a duduk, the woodwind instrument he had previously played on 2004's "Jenny Wren".

Paul McCartney – vocals, electric piano, harmonium, triangle,
    congas, acoustic guitar, electric guitar, bird recording
Greg Kurstin – electric piano, bass FX
Abe Laboriel, Jr. – drums, backing vocals
Pedro Eustache – duduk, bamboo flute

212. WHO CARES
Paul McCartney

Written by Paul McCartney
Recorded 2017
Released December 17, 2018
Album: EGYPT STATION

Intending to write a song that would speak to younger people, Paul had taken note of the strong connection between Taylor Swift and her fans, many of whom regard her as a big sister. He thought about the problems young people face and knew that bullying is more prevalent than ever thanks to Internet trolling. Paul wrote "Who Cares" to provide them with some musical encouragement.

Similar in message but more emphatic than "Somebody Who Cares" from 1982's *Tug of War*, Paul sings "Who cares what the idiots say? Who cares what the idiots do?" and advises anyone who feels picked on or unacknowledged to recognize their true worth. Each of the choruses ends with the reassuring "Who cares about you? I do."

Released in September 2018, *Egypt Station* became Paul's first #1 album since *Tug of War* and his first ever to debut in that coveted position. December saw an entertaining music video for "Who Cares" produced by Creative Visions, a nonprofit organization that uses the arts to promote social change. In conjunction with the video, Paul launched the anti-bullying campaign #WhoCaresIDo.

In the short film, Oscar winner Emma Stone visits the office of a "behavioral hypnotist meteorologist" played by a bespectacled Paul. After mesmerizing his patient, he helps her exorcise a group of dancing mimes harassing her. Paul hoped that the humor of the video would help kids laugh off their abusers.

Paul McCartney – vocals, acoustic guitar, bass
Rusty Anderson – electric guitar, backing vocals
Brian Ray – electric guitar, backing vocals
Paul "Wix" Wickens – Farfisa and Hammond organs
Abe Laboriel, Jr. – drums, backing vocals

213. CAESAR ROCK
Paul McCartney

Written by Paul McCartney
Recorded 2017
Released July 2019
Album: EGYPT STATION

As with many modern-day McCartney songs, "Caesar Rock" was created in the studio, building up tracks from scratch. Paul often speaks of the feeling of freedom it affords to not be confined to doing a premeditated composition. The lyrics are actually "She's a rock," but Paul started referring to it as "Caesar Rock" and it stuck.

One of Paul's favorites on *Egypt Station*, it was released as a single in Brazil. The funk-rock song's eclectic characteristics include Paul's nearly unrecognizable growling lead vocal (akin to that heard on "Monkberry Moon Delight" from *Ram*), backwards guitars, and some minor 6th riffs of the Prince variety. The Linn drum machine that opens the song reflects the original tempo Paul had in mind for the song, which abruptly shifts into its slower counterpart.

For the last verse, Paul grabbed people hanging around the studio to do a call and response with him, shouting out random qualities of the woman praised in "Caesar Rock": "She got loyalty (like the royalty), she got symmetry (anonymity), she got all the looks (she got all the books)." Closing out the song is one last adlibbed virtue: "She got matching teeth!" Paul doesn't even remember saying it, but he liked it so much that he considered naming the album *Matching Teeth*.

Paul McCartney – vocals, acoustic guitar, harpsichord, synthesizer, bass, drums, percussion
Rusty Anderson – reverse electric guitar, backing vocals
Brian Ray – electric guitar, backing vocals
Paul "Wix" Wickens – Moog, backing vocals
Abe Laboriel, Jr. – drums, backing vocals
Roy Bennett – backing vocals
Caroline Le'gene – backing vocals

214. GET ENOUGH
Paul McCartney

Written by Paul McCartney and Ryan Tedder
Recorded 2017
Released January 1, 2019
Album: EGYPT STATION (Explorer's Edition)

Ringing in 2019—at the very stroke of midnight—Paul surprised fans online with a new single that had received no advance publicity. "Get Enough" was one of the three songs he had co-written and produced with Ryan Tedder during the *Egypt Station* sessions but were only included on special editions of the CD.

From the mid-'60s onward, no two Beatle songs sounded alike. Throughout his solo career, Paul continued to keep variety upfront via ever-changing instrumentation and arrangements. The concept behind *Egypt Station*, in fact, was to take listeners on an audio journey—a "headphones-for-an-hour trip"—opening with the sounds of a train depot and traveling to different musical experiences. Paul resisted calling it a concept album, even though he had helped invent the genre.

21st century studio tricks abound on "Get Enough". The piano ballad makes liberal use of Auto-Tune, which Paul had been experimenting with due to recent studio work with Kanye West. Paul initially resisted using Auto-Tune, thinking such audio manipulation was somehow sacrilegious, until he reminded himself that the Beatles were all about experimentation. In the case of "Get Enough", beyond merely fine-tuning the pitch, the plugin transformed the vocals into something otherworldly and robotic.

Its wistful lyrics recall pledging his heart to a long-lost lover, professing that her memory lingers and he still can't get enough of her love. Upon bursting into a Beach Boys-like bridge, wordless harmonies passionately overpower an indiscernible spoken passage.

Paul McCartney – vocals, piano, acoustic guitar, bass, harpsichord, synth bass
Ryan Tedder – backing vocals

215. NOTHING FOR FREE
Paul McCartney

Written by Paul McCartney and Ryan Tedder
Recorded 2017
Released May 19, 2019
Album: EGYPT STATION (Explorer's Edition)

OneRepublic's Ryan Tedder, Paul's most recent songwriting and producing collaborator, admitted he wasn't a Beatles fan until he bought a car in which the previous owner had left a CD of the White Album. After listening to it, Tedder was hooked and collected all the Beatle albums. The hit-making producer for Adele, Beyoncé, Maroon 5 and many others came to realize that his dream gig was to someday work with Paul McCartney.

In time, alerted by Paul's manager that he could expect a call from Paul, Tedder was elated, but weeks went by and it left his mind. He was having lunch at a restaurant when he finally got the call. Seeing an unknown number with a foreign country code, Tedder ignored it. His phone rang again, and Tedder continued to dismiss it. After yet a third go-round, he got a text asking if he was free to talk. Tedder texted back, "New number, who dis?" He sprung into action when the reply came back: "Sir Paul."

Meeting Paul for the first time, Tedder said, was nerve-wracking. He prayed beforehand that he wouldn't embarrass himself and would display enough talent to pull off working with the icon. For his part, Paul expressed appreciation that hot young producers like Tedder wanted to collaborate with him.

The third single they co-wrote, "Nothing for Free", boasts a strong Tedder imprint, from the sampled vocal snippets to the leaping melody in its hook. Tedder said he was "beyond happy" to have been able to work with Paul and that it was his favorite week of all time.

Paul McCartney – vocals, electric guitar, acoustic guitar, piano, harpsichord, synthesizer, bass
Ryan Tedder – backing vocals

216. WHAT'S MY NAME
Ringo Starr

Written by Colin Hay
Recorded 2019
Released September 13, 2019
Album: WHAT'S MY NAME

Not everyone can get away with singing about themselves, much less using their own name in the chorus, but fans at Ringo's All-Starr Band concerts know that a frequent exchange between Ringo and his audiences is, "What's my name?" "RINGO!" Once he has introduced all the other members of his band, there isn't much left to say other than that, and the crowd eats it up.

All-Starr Band regular (and former Men at Work frontman) Colin Hay wrote this rollicking rocker in which Ringo recalls his six-decade career. Hay composed the song six years earlier but had put it aside. When Ringo got wind of it from another musician, he asked to hear it but Hay couldn't remember where he'd put it. The song was eventually found in the bottom of a drawer.

Sticking to his proven formula of an all-star lineup, *What's My Name*—Ringo's 20th album—features collaborations with Joe Walsh, Edgar Winter, Steve Lukather, Dave Stewart, and many other rock notables.

Calling it "the smallest club in town," Ringo's Beverly Hills home studio was specifically designed to be a comfortable place where he and his musician friends could make music without the isolating aspects of the big glass barrier typical of traditional studios. Inviting friends into his home, Ringo says, is "good for me and for the music."

Ringo Starr – vocals, drums, percussion
Colin Hay – guitar, backing vocals
Steve Lukather – guitar
Nathan East – bass
Warren Ham – harmonica
Maxine Waters, Julie Waters – backing vocals

217. GROW OLD WITH ME
Ringo Starr

Written by John Lennon
Recorded 2019
Released October 11, 2019
Album: WHAT'S MY NAME

During John Lennon's Bermuda vacation in the summer of 1980, he and Yoko wrote songs independently and played them to each other over the phone. One of Yoko's songs ("Let Me Count the Ways") was based on a sonnet by Elizabeth Barrett Browning, and Yoko suggested that John write one around a Robert Browning poem.

As fate would have it, John saw an old movie on TV that very day in which the main character receives a poem called "Rabbi Ben Ezra", written by none other than Robert Browning. Within hours, he phoned Yoko in New York and played her "Grow Old with Me". The song borrows the first two lines of the 1864 poem: "Grow old along with me, the best is yet to be." One of John's demos was posthumously released in 1984, and quickly became a popular wedding song.

Ringo said he was prompted to record "Grow Old with Me" after hearing John's original Bermuda demo, on which John says, "This would be a great one for you, Ringo." John's own producer Jack Douglas did Ringo's string arrangement, while Paul contributes bass and backing vocals. Low in the mix at 3:02, Ringo says, "God bless you, John."

Ringo Starr – vocals, drums
Paul McCartney – bass, backing vocals
Joe Walsh – guitar
Jim Cox – piano
Allison Lovejoy – accordion
Rhea Fowler – violin
Bianca McClure – violin
Lauren Baba – viola
Isaiah Cage – cello

218. LIFE IS GOOD
Ringo Starr

Written by Richard Starkey and Gary Burr
Recorded 2019
Released October 25, 2019
Album: WHAT'S MY NAME

In 1994, after designing their first "Life is Good" t-shirt, Bert and John Jacobs found that their positive message resonated with the masses. Today, Life is Good shirts are sold in over 4,000 stores. The philanthropic brothers stage charity events and are the authors of *Life is Good: The Book – How to Live with Purpose and Enjoy the Ride.*

The Jacobses sent Ringo a copy of their book, which he received the same week he and Gary Burr got together to write a new song. Ringo spotted the cover and used the title as a prompt for "Life is Good". In turn, the Jacobs brothers collaborated with Ringo and designed a special shirt in conjunction with his 79th birthday.

Every July 7th, Ringo celebrates another year via a Peace & Love event in a different city, asking people around the world to join him in sending out positive vibes. The 11th annual commemoration in 2019 took place in Los Angeles with the Jacobses on hand plus local bands and students of the John Lennon Educational Tour Bus.

The king of musical pep talks began his 30th anniversary All-Starr Band tour three weeks later. Before going on the road, Ringo and the band only needed a day and a half of rehearsals versus the typical two weeks because they had worked so well together for so many years. As Ringo rejoiced, "A little help from my friends has become a reality."

Ringo Starr – vocals, drums, percussion
Steve Lukather – guitar
Benmont Tench – organ
Bruce Sugar – synthesizer
Nathan East – bass
Richard Page, Warren Ham, Windy Wager, Kari Kimmel – backing
 vocals

219. HOME TONIGHT
Paul McCartney

Written by Paul McCartney
Recorded 2018
Released November 22, 2019
Digital download

Record Store Day is an annual event traditionally held twice a year in which independent record stores are the only sellers of exclusive new releases. Among the Black Friday November 2019 offerings for collectors was a double-sided vinyl single by Paul, consisting of "Home Tonight" and "In a Hurry". Both songs were recorded during the *Egypt Station* sessions with Greg Kurstin but were not included on the album. The songs were also made available a week prior to Record Store Day via digital download.

Not to be confused with "If I Take You Home Tonight"—also written by Paul and appearing on Diana Krall's *Wallflower* album— the upbeat "Home Tonight" does at least share a similar sentiment. He is reassuring someone that, if he takes them home, he will look after their best interests. In this case it's to protect them from cold winds coming and to generally make sure they're alright. The joyous, bass-driven beat with a brassy backdrop is an ironic contrast to lyrics lamenting a world that's falling apart to the point where he can't find the tears.

The limited-edition 7" picture disc featured cover art by the London illustrators who patterned *Egypt Station* after a 1988 painting of Paul's by the same name. The design for "Home Tonight" was inspired by a drawing game called Exquisite Corpse, in which diverse body parts come together to create grotesque figures.

Paul McCartney – vocals, guitars, bass, drums, hand claps
Steve Herrman – trumpet
Tom "Bones" Malone – bass trombone, tenor saxophone, trumpet
Charles Rose – trombone
Jim Hoke – baritone saxophone
Doug Moffett – tenor saxophone

220. IN A HURRY
Paul McCartney

Written by Paul McCartney
Recorded 2018
Released November 22, 2019
Digital download

The flip side of the double-sided Record Store Day single with "Home Tonight" was the fanciful "In a Hurry", a song full of familiar McCartney DNA. Rich harmonies, tempo changes, sound effects of a concert crowd, and a false ending add inventive touches to a presentation that would have been right at home on *Sgt. Pepper*.

A simple but stylish bass and calliope-like keyboard intro leads into an observational lyric about a woman who's been too busy taking care of duty to take care of herself. After Paul admonishes her to find the laughter she's looking for, the song picks up in double time and bursts into triumphant choruses reinforcing that it's "never too late to celebrate."

Paul's touring band is on hand, but mostly just to sing harmony. The basic track was performed by Paul and producer Greg Kurstin, embellished by a 40-piece orchestra combining members of the Los Angeles Philharmonic and the Hollywood Bowl Orchestra. All of the available studio engineers joined Paul and Kurstin to do hand claps.

> Paul McCartney – vocals, piano, harpsichord, harmonium, acoustic guitar, electric guitar, slide guitar, bass, drums, hand claps
> Greg Kurstin – piano, vibraphone, synthesizer, Moog bass, hand claps
> Paul "Wix" Wickens – piano
> Abe Laboriel, Jr. – drums, tambourine, backing vocals
> Brian Ray – backing vocals
> Rusty Anderson – backing vocals
> Jim Hoke – baritone saxophone, harmonica
> Brad Giroux, Julian Burg, Keith Smith, Matt Tuggle, Steve Orchard – hand claps

AND IN THE END

Five decades after their breakup, the Beatles continue to amass new fans and maintain the faithful. Paul and Ringo show no signs of slowing down, and the families of John and George ably carry the mantle, ensuring that their legacy lives on.

Since 1969, the iconic Abbey Road crosswalk has been traversed by countless millions of pedestrians seeking their own walk of fame. Consequently, the paint on the zebra crossing looked pretty run down by March 2020 when the COVID-19 shutdown slowed traffic on Abbey Road to a crawl. Taking a sad song and making it better, a London maintenance crew used the downtime to give the national landmark a much celebrated touchup.

In April 2020, more than 250 items of Beatle memorabilia were auctioned off online via Julien's Auctions in New York. An ashtray used by Ringo at Abbey Road Studios went for $32,500. A drawing by John yielded $93,750. A drumhead with The Beatles' logo fetched $200,000, and Paul's handwritten lyrics to "Hey Jude" were sold for $910,000. As for the highest-priced Beatles lyrics of all time, the record is still held by "All You Need is Love", which at a 2005 auction went for $1.25 million.

Glastonbury Festival is a major performing arts event held each summer in Somerset, England. Paul was to be headliner in June 2020 and teased the announcement on Twitter by posting images of Philip Glass, Emma Stone and Chuck Berry side by side in a sly rebus of Glass/Stone/Berry. The coronavirus pandemic forced the cancellation of the festival, but when it resumes in 2021, it's likely to recreate the lineup that also includes Kendrick Lamar and Taylor Swift.

Paul's 2020 Freshen Up Tour dates were also canceled. Said Paul, "We were looking forward to seeing you this summer for what we know would have been much fun. The band and I are so sorry we can't be with you, but these are unprecedented times and the well-being and safety of everyone is the priority. I hope you are keeping well as we look forward to brighter times ahead. We will rock again. Love, Paul."

With a little luck, 2021 could see the opening of the stage musical *It's a Wonderful Life*, with music and lyrics by Sir Paul. The most popular Christmas movie of all time takes to the footlights at the hands of Lee Hall, creator of *Billy Elliot* and screenwriter for the Elton John biopic *Rocketman*. Hall says "Paul's wit, emotional honesty and melodic brilliance brings a whole new depth and breadth to the classic tale. The songs sound simple but it's deceptive. That's Paul's genius."

2020 will bring a variety of John Lennon tributes. October 9 would have been his 80th birthday, and December 8 marks the 40th anniversary of his death. A commemorative promotion of his 1970 album *Plastic Ono Band* is likely in the fall, along with a documentary called *John Lennon: The Final Year* with never-before-seen archive footage and interviews with those who were part of his life in 1980. Among its producers is Ken Womack, author of *John Lennon 1980: The Final Days in the Life of Beatle John*, which is scheduled to be published on John's birthday.

Drivers in Florida and California get to "imagine there's no hunger" by sporting an Imagine license plate featuring John's artwork. With options ranging from $50 to $199, the special plates have raised millions of dollars to support area food banks. It is hoped that drivers in other states will eventually get the same opportunity while they're watching the wheels.

George's Material World Foundation, which he started in 1973, continues to support charities and causes around the world. Under Olivia and Dhani's direction, in 2020 it donated $500,000 to the MusiCares COVID-19 Relief Fund, Save the Children, and Doctors without Borders.

To raise additional funds for coronavirus relief, the foundation staged The Inner Light Challenge, donating up to another $100,000 on behalf of everyone sharing their "inner light" on social media. A dollar was added to the fund for each person posting something inspired by George's song "The Inner Light" using the hashtag #innerlight2020. Celebrities who participated via video include Jeff Lynne, Jewel, Mick Fleetwood, Paul Rodgers and Susanna Hoffs.

Ringo said his 2019 album, *What's My Name*, may be his last, though he doesn't intend to stop recording. Future releases are likely to be EPs of three songs rather than entire albums.

His next All-Starr Band tour of North America, postponed from 2020, is scheduled to begin in Ontario in May 2021 and work its way down the East Coast to Florida in June. Meanwhile, readers are enjoying *Another Day in the Life*, Ringo's third book of previously unpublished photographs and personal anecdotes.

Seen regularly at a popular California juice bar, Ringo remains fit and slender even as he steps lightly into his 80s. He says he stays healthy by doing Pilates and eating a lot of broccoli.

Scheduled for August 27, 2021 is the theatrical release of the long-awaited Peter Jackson documentary *The Beatles: Get Back*. With full blessing from Paul, Ringo, Olivia and Yoko, the *Lord of the Rings* filmmaker has revisited 55 hours of footage and 140 hours of recording sessions to create a much more positive take on the original *Let It Be* film (which has also been restored and will be released separately).

Those who have previewed Jackson's new film have remarked of its pristine restoration quality and a stellar soundtrack mixed by Giles Martin. *Get Back* is praised for being a joyful experience that refutes the long-held belief that the Beatles' *Let It Be* days were all bad. Ringo confirms this retrospective is "a lot more peace and loving, like we really were." Paul sums it up: "The friendship and love between us comes across and reminds us of what a crazily beautiful time we had."

❖

ALPHA SONG INDEX

Made in United States
North Haven, CT
04 January 2022

14180319R00134